Beckett's English Poetry

Transcending the Roots of Resistance in Language

Beckett's English Poetry

Transcending the Roots of Resistance in Language

A. V. Koshy

AUTHORSPRESS

Worldwide Circulation through Authorspress Global Network

First Published 2013

by

Authorspress

Editorial

Q-2A Hauz Khas Enclave

New Delhi-110 016

Marketing

E-35/103, Jawahar Park

Laxmi Nagar, Delhi-110 092

e-mails: authorspress@rediffmail.com; authorspress@hotmail.com

Website: www.authorspressbooks.com

Beckett's English Poetry: Transcending the Roots of Resistance in Language

ISBN 978-81-7273-722-1

Printed in India at Krishna Offset, Shahdara.

Dedicated to my mother Sara, my inspiration,
who was herself a writer and poet.

Contents

Preface

Samuel Barclay Beckett was born in Foxrock, Dublin, Ireland. His parents were Protestants, having French Huguenot ancestors. His father, William Beckett, was a quantity surveyor. His mother Mary Beckett, also called May, had a puritanical disposition and taught Beckett the Bible. Bill, her husband, was more easy-going. Beckett had an elder brother called Frank. 'Sam' gradually grew away from his family, although his comfortable middle-class upbringing was not one to give him cause for complaint. He outlived all the members of his family and the grief caused by the separation of death appears frequently in his works. Beckett's date of birth, he said, was April 13, 1906, a Good Friday. But this story has not been supported by his biographer Deirdre Bair.[1] It might be a fiction that he foisted on himself in keeping with his image as the writer with the bleakest vision in twentieth-century literature. Beckett studied in Portora Royal High School, Ulster, and Trinity College, Dublin. He was interested in chess, cricket, rugby and golf. His appreciation of these, especially chess, manifests itself in the works "For Future Reference," *Murphy*, *Endgame* and "The Three Dialogues" with Georges Duthuit.

Beckett grasped the complexities of the structures of Western classical music well. He had a talent for languages and a love of literature that helped him to master French, German and Italian literature. He added Spanish to this list later, besides having a smattering of Greek and Latin. He was "a polyglot punster"[2] and hence words from languages as diverse as Hebrew and Sanskrit appear in his works. He won a gold medal for brilliance in his studies and, as expected, became a teacher. His friend Arthur Rudmose-Brown introduced him to the modern French poets like Arthur Rimbaud, Charles Baudelaire, Stephen Mallarmé and Paul Valéry who changed the perception of the best poets of his time. They influenced W.B. Yeats, T.S. Eliot, Ezra Pound etc., deeply. But Beckett was more fascinated by the lesser known, more 'avant-garde' poets like Jules Romains, the Unanimist, and Guillaume Apollinaire, the first Surrealist. Beckett's Continental visits brought him in touch with James Joyce who was then in France. He wrote a monograph on Marcel Proust that was appreciated in academic circles, a few poems, pieces of criticism and short stories. He fell in love with Peggy Sinclair; a cousin of his who had green eyes, was Irish-German and died young of tuberculosis. Her death inspired him to write his first 'enueg' poems. He had sexual liaisons, seemingly, with women like 'the Alba Perdue' of the early short stories and *Dream of Fair to Middling Women*. He eventually resigned his job as a lecturer.

The early years of his life went by in wandering, drinking heavily, learning to appreciate painting, cinema and theatre, being ill and poor, attempting journalism, writing creative pieces sporadically, receiving little attention from the critics and being published only in small literary magazines. His father's death in June 1933 was a rude shock to him. The poem "Malacoda" commemorates the occasion. His father left him a slender but steady income that helped him to continue his writing career. Around 1937, in Paris a pimp stabbed Beckett and later when asked why by him he said "Je ne sais pas, Monsieur" (I don't know, Mister).[3] The answer became central to Beckett's writings. Suzanne Dumesnil who eventually became his wife came into his life at this time. Beckett's knowledge of the other fine arts and his deep knowledge in general increased rapidly. During the Second World War he joined the French Resistance, against Hitler's Nazi Germany and anti-Semitic madness, risking his life. He avoided arrest, went into hiding and wrote Watt. He won a Croix de Guerre for bravery and worked for a little while, after the war, as a translator for the Red Cross to help the rehabilitation of bombed cities like Saint-Lô. By this time his friends included not only Irish artists like Jack. B. Yeats and Thomas MacGreevey but also Henri Haydn, Avigdor Arikha and the van Velde brothers, Geer and Bram.

Beckett's period of greatness as a writer began after all this. His writing prowess exploded, helped along by the fear that a tumour in his cheek was cancerous and could result in death. The fear turned out to be false. But many of the books that he wrote then during 1946-'50, including *Waiting for Godot* and *The Unnamable*, have become classics of world literature. When *Waiting for Godot* was produced by Roger Blin it instantly became noticed by leading critics like Jean Cocteau. To paraphrase Hugh Kenner, just as in the thirties everyone inhabited the 'Waste Land ' in the fifties all waited for 'Godot'.[4]

Beckett's personal life became less and less momentous. But as the years went by, in the midst of his busy aesthetic life of play-direction, writing, creation and translation his loved ones and friends kept slipping away from him. 1950 saw the death of his mother. In "Footfalls" and *Ill Seen Ill Said* Beckett pays oblique tribute to her.

Beckett died on December 22, 1989, in the week before Christmas. His fame has remained unshaken. The recent publication of *Dream of Fair to Middling Women* has again sparked off controversial interest in his talent. *Eleutheria,* his first completed and 'unstaged' play, is also now published. So is much else that he has written. Some early pieces like the short stories "Assumption," "A Case in a Thousand" and "Echo's Bones" are not read by the present reader.

In 1961 Beckett shared, with the equally great Argentine author Jorge Luis Borges, the Prix Formentor prize for writing. Both of them went on to win the Nobel Prize for Literature. Beckett received the prize in 1969. Unlike in some other cases, no one questioned his right to be granted this prestigious award. Beckett's art has been labelled Modern, Cartesian, Nihilist, Existentialist, Absurd etc., according to the changing critical mores and times. At present it is considered as one of the best examples of the post-modern, deconstructive, super-structural literary epoch we live in. His ability to move ahead of the Zeitgeist did not prevent him from being 'satiric' and 'apocalyptic' in his vision like his Puritan ancestors.

Although not "a political animal,"[5] Beckett was one of the writers who consistently involved himself in the fight against literary censorship and human tyranny. He spoke out on behalf of Fernando Arrabal and Vaclav Havel in the days of their imprisonment under Communist regimes. More recently, he was among those who deplored the threat on Salman Rushdie's life. In a sense he continued to be part of an invisible Resistance that opposed all forms of literary or human censorship or dictatorship. Beckett had no children in keeping with his strange view that procreation is a crime. His works, however, survive him with a vengeance.

The following book is perhaps intended primarily for third-world readers who are already quite familiar with Beckett's life, the available works in English and a substantial amount of the criticism on them. Hence biographical details appear rarely, only when essential to the interpretation. Since Lawrence E. Harvey has already done a minute detailed study of most of Beckett's poems written before 1950 in his book *Samuel Beckett: Poet and Critic*, the effort has been not so much the exposition of all the twists and turns of the poems but the extension of the readings. A more holistic approach has been attempted, made possible by the spadework other critics have done in this area. This study does not deal with Beckett's French writings and translations like "the Huit Maximes/After Chamfort" or the French poems. Considering Beckett as an English poet has involved a questionable division of his texts on a chronological generic basis, but the clarity and consistency gained consequently in the conclusion of the book is, one hopes, a sufficient gain to offset this. The word 'poem' has been thought of as being adequately defined by tradition and hence Beckett's excursions into regions that break this norm have been neglected. The lack of space in which to accommodate everything is another important reason for such omissions. The French poems without translations, the transcreations, the lineated drama "Rockaby" (a lullaby), the hybrid play "What Where," Beckett's free-prose pieces like "Texts for Nothing" and "Fizzles" that can be called prose poems by a stretch of the imagination, his "lyrics of criticism"[6] on Avigdor Arikha, Jack. B. Yeats, Henri Haydn etc., in *Disjecta* have all been left untouched in the 'formal' context as territory those who follow can explore. But the startling depth of the poems in English has ensured that the study is still sufficiently multi-layered. No attempt has been made to compare and contrast the poems with those of others, often, because such an imposition would look forced and would not fit in with the drift of the main argument, becoming instead a sub- theme having too much importance to be woven neatly in with the other. Wherever Beckett uses as his 'source' texts in languages other than English, authentic commentaries have been depended on instead of originals that are not understandable or translations that are not available. In compensation of these short-comings this book can point to the fact that it is the first on Beckett's poems to study all of his published English poems including the ones omitted by Harvey and the snippets of verse in his prose texts, thus up-dating Harvey's seminal work on Beckett's poems and poetics beyond the fifties into the nineties. As a thematic study dealing with the question of Beckettian semantics in connection with the poems the present work tries to clarify Beckett's position further; a task more feasible now since the author ceased from writing in 1987 and his work is beginning to take on a definite parabola retrospectively.

The brief introduction to this book states the background of Beckett's poems and traces out, vestigially, the development of his poetic graph. It divides Beckett's poems into two periods. "The years of learning"[7] can be called the former half of the early period of 1929-'35. Beckett wrote his "jettisoned poems"[8] then. They are juvenile and imitative, yet passable. The second half of the early phase is that of "the years of wandering."[9] They show Beckett as a representative, typical modern poet who could occasionally be jejune or brilliant. They also reveal his avant-garde posture and show him moving on rapidly to Post-modernism. The poems of the first collection *Echo's Bones* are the ones of this latter half of the early period. The second or mature period of Beckett's poetic career stretches from 1935 to his death with a stretch of long silence (e.g., 1950 - '73) in between. In this phase his style became distinct and, from Watt onwards, post-structural. The poems reflect "deceleration" and perpetrate or perpetuate very few aesthetic blunders. His restless inventiveness in the matters of form, structure and themes is mentioned. The elusive depth he generates in his poems is hinted at. Stock is taken of the details that matter (i.e., facts, feats, figures, dates, names, places etc.) and the influences and affinities that ought to be known.

The first chapter on the years of learning analyses the first twelve of Beckett's available poems in English that he later considered immature, except perhaps for "Whoroscope." The sections where he equals or rivals his mentors, then living or dead, like Browning, Dante, Joyce, Eliot etc., are highlighted. His wrestling with the issue of whether eroticism, Christianity or art should be chosen as a way of life is seen as the thread that unites these disparate exercises. Beckett gives up his youthful interest in sex and is shown as opting for art as his religion, without a corresponding faith that it will lead him to any sort of redemption. "Whoroscope" and "Gnome," the finer poems of this period, are studied in some detail. The second chapter on the years of wandering dissects the thirteen poems in *Echo's Bones*. Beckett's modernity, existentialism and nihilistic tendencies etc., are explored. The poems sparkle with compressed metaphoric gems of youthful lustre in a manner not found in any of his other works. The well- nigh inexhaustible nature of the collection, its allusive flexibility and the obscurities that become transparent to the patient eye are all meditated on. The fine touches in the poems and the better poems like "The Vulture" and "Da Tagte Es" are investigated. The aesthetically viable claim that the collection is a 'sequence' is established in the course of the chapter.

In the third chapter the even excellence of most of Beckett's poems of the mature phase from 1935 is contemplated. Beckett's move towards a metaphysical and aesthetic poetry that is implicitly 'minimal' is noticed. The insights that are thrown up in the process are sometimes 'new' and may help to explain strange Beckettian texts like "dread nay" and "Something there" to the reader for the first time. The generally high standard of the poems being studied has led to the chapter being called "the blue celeste of poesy."[10]

The conclusion, besides explaining the theme of the book, i.e., the bridled anguish of non-expression, by which Beckett 'transcends the roots of resistance in language,' also sums up the poet's achievements. Beckett's technical, formal, structural and thematic concerns are stated and illustrated point by point. His major theme or semantic structure of meaning, one that deconstructs itself in its attempt to be 'knowing' and is borrowed from the Hegelian dialectic, is laid bare. Its vicissitudes, as they appear throughout the many poems as the pair 'Being' and 'Nothingness' in metaphors, are traced out. The deduction is that Beckett's deep metaphysical base, although not fully critique-resistant, places him on an ontologically valid aesthetic path that few have thought of as existing before or trod. His resultant fear of failure is shown as being stemmed by solitary moments of poetic transcendence that come his way more and more frequently over the years. These moments are also, incidentally, among the best in the history of English poetry of the twentieth century, according to the present writer.

Giving thanks where it is due, the glory belongs to the Lord Jesus Christ. I thank Dr. K. Radha, then HoD of the Institute of English, TVPM, Kerala, whose valuable guidance made this book possible. Her constant encouragement, her patience, the suggestions she gave with regard to the subject and the corrections she made to improve the manuscript helped me to complete this book. The research work for this book was carried out mainly at the Institute of English, University of Kerala, Thiruvananthapuram. The libraries helpful to my research were the Institute of English library, the B.C.L., the University Library and the Public Library in Trivandrum and the E.F.L.U. Library in Hyderabad. I extend my gratitude to the teachers at the

Institute of English. I also thank the library and office staff for their kind co-operation. I acknowledge the Junior Research Fellowship granted to me long ago by the University Grants Commission through the University of Kerala to help me financially. I express my indebtedness to many friends who encouraged me, prayed for me and helped me in my work with their time and clues. I wish to thank Mr. Ramakrishnan especially, for making my manuscript legible with his skill at typing and his useful tips on how to improve my research methodology. I lovingly thank my parents, both my brothers, my sister and the rest of the family, including the little ones, my nieces and nephews, without whose whole-hearted love, emotional support, prayers, mental and verbal abilities to debate with me meaningfully on the subject, graphic assistance, sacrifices and insistence that I complete, I would not have pulled on or completed this book. I remember the late Aveesh K with gratitude for suggesting the topic to me. Last but not least, I thank Dr. Bina Biswas, for believing in me and helping me and Sudarshan Kcherry for his nobility in publishing my book and supplying the title, despite my artistic temperament and tantrums. I thank George Korah of Primalogue and Jonsy for cleaning the manuscript. I thank Anu, my love and my wife, for loving, supporting and helping me always. I am also grateful to my children for all their love. The sole responsibility for errors, omissions and unacknowledged or unconscious echoes and prejudices rests with me. This book does not purport to extend beyond knowledge gathered beyond 1994, which is its main limitation.

Notes

1. Deirde Bair, *Samuel Beckett: A Biography* (London: Jonathan Cape, 1978) 14.

2. Lawrence E. Harvey, *Samuel Beckett: Poet & Critic* (New Jersey: Princeton U.P., 1970) 58.
3. Martin Esslin, *The Theatre of the Absurd* (England: Penguin, 1983) 36.
4. Hugh Kenner, *A Reader's Guide to Samuel Beckett* (London: Thames & Hudson, 1973) 39.
5. Harvey, *Samuel Beckett*, 135.
6. Ruby Cohn, "Foreword," in Samuel Beckett's Disjecta ed. Ruby Cohn (London: Calder, 1983) 15.
7. Samuel Beckett, "Gnome," *Collected Poems* 1930 - '78 (London: Calder, 1984) 7.
8. Harvey 305.
9. Beckett, "Gnome," *C.P.*, 7.
10. Beckett, "Lessness," *A Samuel Beckett Reader* ed. John Calder (London: Picador, 1983) 262.

A Brief Introduction

Beckett is not only a significant playwright and prosateur but also a sensitive poet of some stature. As John Calder states, "he has . . . written enough verse to be seen as an important poet in his own right ... in English and in French, and he has made some astonishing translations."[1]

The Years of Learning and Wandering

Many of his poems were written during 1929 -'35. They have evoked attention from critics of the calibre of Martin Esslin, Marjorie Perloff, Hugh Kenner, John Fletcher, John Pilling, Donald Davie, Richard Coe and others. Davie and Coe have written reviews that are dismissive of Beckett's early poems. But Lawrence E. Harvey elucidates their vitality and importance, paying an adequate tribute to them in his book *Samuel Beckett: Poet and Critic* (1970).

Regarding his early attempts at writing verse, Esslin says:

> . . . of all of Beckett's writing the slim corpus of his poetry contains his most directly autobiographical utterance. . . Beckett's poems are compressed to the point of being in code: a single line may carry multiple meanings, public and private allusions, description and symbol, topographical references, snatches of overheard conversations, fragments in other languages . . Four lines may thus require four pages of elucidation, provided . . . the full information . . . could ever be elicited.[2]

The points that make a study of these poems imperative are the following. Their opacity and their experimental nature call for clarification. The clues in them of the origins of Beckett's writings lead to excavation. The autobiographical element and the connections of his poems to his other works invite comment. That his poems reveal in embryo dominant literary themes and aesthetic motifs that constantly occupied only Beckett also counts. Finally, the scant critical attention that they have received challenges the present reader to attempt a fuller interpretation.

The early poems reveal that Beckett was influenced by vast sources and diverse people. The Bible, the works and personae of René DesCartes, James Joyce, Dante, Marcel Proust, Arthur Rimbaud, Paul Eluard, Guillaume Apollinaire, Arthur Schopenhauer, Robert Browning, Democritus, Ovid, Goethe, Walther von der Vogelweide, the Provençal and Italian troubadours, the German minnesingers and Graeco-Roman mythology need special mention in this context. The presence of echoes in his poems of those of Novalis, J.C.F Hölderlin, Wordsworth and Pierre de Ronsard suggests his ties with Romanticism. But his sombre tone is not necessarily Romantic in origin. The influences on Beckett are innumerable. The appearance of techniques like allusiveness, arbitrariness and associativeness shows the effect of the many art-movements like Surrealism[3] that were a part of his time on him. The resistance his early verse offers to lineation and his scrambling of punctuation-marks are small-scale denominators that exemplify this. His language —'signifiers' running riot in unstable contexts — was initially Joycean. Jazz rhythms and the writing of aubades and serenades reflect his knowledge of music. The similarity of some of his poems to Ezra Pound's and T.S Eliot's is clear. Hopkinsian compounds and Joycean neologisms are not unusual. Surrealistic images as startling as any in Dylan Thomas's poems, albeit substantially different and fewer in number, are not uncommon.

Beckett's penchant was for free verse, in keeping with his appreciation of the European avant-garde. His poems, form-wise, were imitative. Hence they were experimental and representative of Modernism. It is recognised that his muse was essentially lyrical. Yet his early poems were prosaic. "Whoroscope" (1930) is a hybrid that consists of free verse and prose notes like *The Waste Land* (1921). Fletcher points out that many of his poems are narrative in structure.[4] Often they are interior or dramatic psychological monologues in the first person. Perloff notes that they meander consistently and the motif being explored is that of the journey and/or the voyage with all the semantic possibilities such a theme incurs.[5] Beckett's use of lists as a form for his poems *(e.g.,* "Enueg I") is noteworthy. His love of the pithy poem as illustrated by the epigram, the proverb, the riddle etc., needs mention in any description of his approach to form. Pilling observes that many of his poems are "occasional"[6] poems, written for or because of an occasion. "Malacoda," written after Beckett's father's death, is an example.

Beckett's poems are ambiguous, ironic, arcane and obfuscatory labyrinths. Linear, circular and spiral patterns recur frequently in them. Artistic, metaphysical, mythical, geographic, psychological, historic and theological strataeform their substance.

Several faults mar his early attempts to write in "the virtuoso mode"[7] of Modernism. Multilingualism and literary allusiveness as a kind of exhibitionism are among them. His excessive verbal pyrotechnics of the Joycean variety often fails. The use of obscenity without purpose and the self-gratuitous introduction of private references and symbols are other irritants. These flaws hinder the amalgamation of form and content. His potential is not fully tapped and its concrete appearance seldom sustained throughout each work. The many influences he imbibed are not properly assimilated and the result is, except in a few poems, tedious or superficial. The early poems are examples of Modernism at an impasse.

David Hayman's seems a balanced estimate of Beckett as a young writer of prose and verse. He comments:

> ... the early prose and verse were predictive. The poems, so admirably studied by Harvey, push beyond Eliot in their disjunct concision, oblique allusions, in the simplicity of their discourse larded with arcane language and in their gestural precision ... the by-now familiar themes already evident ... the sexual and scatologic wit put to clearly anti-poetic uses ... here and elsewhere Beckett displays his adherence to latest trends; and indeed his extension of them in what must be seen as a young-man's effort to outdo as well as épater (flatten).[8]

He adds:

> The early poetry and prose both display weaknesses, such as the occasional lapse into leaden wit or the self-conscious aping of a too-much admired Joyce.[9]

Of the jettisoned poems, especially "Hell Crane to Starling" (1931), Beckett said that they were the exercises of a "young man with nothing to say and the itch to make."[10] "Whoroscope" remains for most critics the significant landmark among them. Kenner states that the collection Echo*'s Bones* (pub. 1935) constitutes the only early work Beckett valued.[11] The early Beckett did create poems like" Yoke of Liberty" (1931), not to mention the even excellence of "The Vulture" and "Da Tagte Es" in *Echo's Bones,* that prefigure his poetic genius fully.

The Blue Celeste of Poesy

On the subject of the early poems, short or long, Kenner mentions that Beckett did not master the ability "to work in the very brief time of a poem, making the elements cohere and suggest"[12] quickly. But he adds that talent soon asserted itself and the better poems "grow very quietly in the mind earning their strangely gentle apocalypse there."[13] Kenner's statement is about "Saint-Lô" (1946) but what he says holds good for most of the poems written by Beckett after 1935.

Beckett's art was in a state of transition between 1936 and '45. He shifted from writing in English to French. The change brought about perceptible differences. In his poetry he shed influences and the irksome habit of allusiveness for a sparse style. The diction and mode become recognizable as his own. The effort to eliminate the unnecessary, allowing the form to become flexible and capable of layers of significance, gains strength. Beckettian traits like his love of repetition and variation surface and begin to receive their focii. Of the English poems written in this phase "Cascando" (1936), "Dieppe" (1937) and one in *Watt* (1945) stand witness to Beckett's arrival as a poet who could, "when the fit seized him [,] ... write a lyric."[14] The quotidian self is replaced by the quintessential. Paradox, indeterminacy and plurality dominate these poems that are enigmatically transparent.

In 1945, for four fertile years Beckett turned away from journalism, book reviewing and the short story to concentrate on the greater possibilities the novella, the anti-novel and the drama offered him. He completed the classics "First Love," "The Expelled," "The Calmative," "The End," *Molloy*, *Malone Dies*. *The Unnamable*, "Texts for Nothing," "*Waiting for Godot*," "The Three Dialogues" and "Six Poémes 1947-'49." The latter is his second collection of poems in French, the first being "Poémes

1937-'39." Two of the poems of 1937-'39 were translated and three of the six poems appear in English also. This massive burst of writing followed Beckett's multi-dimensional experiences during the Second World War. In an interview with Israel Shenker in 1956 he said:

> I wrote all my work very fast between 1946 and 1950. Since then I haven't written anything ...that has seemed to me valid.[15]

But one must not always trust the teller totally.

> The important poems in English that belong to this period are "Saint-Lô" and the translations. They are lucid lyrical pieces that remind one of the fine paintings of Surrealists like Salvador Dali. They consequently draw forth complimentary reactions from the critics.

What happened to Beckett the versateur in 1950-'73 is perhaps best explained in borrowed words. To quote Esslin again:

> Beckett ... stopped writing verse. But occasionally the voices [in his works] themselves speak inverse. And that verse is as concise, as economical, as profound and essential as Beckett's personal poetry.[16]

The two poems in the radio-play "Words and Music" (1962) are the examples.

Beckett no longer felt the urge to write verse for a long while. In his initial attempts at creative writing he constantly chose verse or the short story as his medium. His first important creative work, it is appropriate to recollect, was "Whoroscope." This hankering to create song may have had as cause, apart from the necessity for brevity, the illusion that poetry has the power to penetrate the surface of things to the core of Heideggerian 'Being.' Later, through experience of the faulty nature of the poetic process, this belief seems to have evaporated. Beckett countered it by letting what is poetic seep into the very fabric of his prose. The alchemy led to a long silence in which he wrote no new verse from 1950 to '73, except for the two poems last mentioned.

The poems Beckett wrote towards the end (1974-'89), though few in number as usual, foreground his increasing concern with form (-lessness) and meaning (-lessness) along with his other works of the time. Minimalism,[17] the postmodern, uncertainty and incompleteness play their share in them. The lyric is extended and subverted. Cartesian dualism is partly deconstructed. The self becomes a nearly impersonal, perceiving voice that mainly perceives itself. But the voice is still recognisable because of the unmistakable ideolect as Beckettian. His style of the period has been compared to that of the Mannerist[18] painters.

His writing of this phase has been called the "literature of exhaustion,"[19] "metalanguage"[20] etc. In these last poems Beckett moves towards a simplicity and clarity of vision that has become both expressible and communicable. His poems remain markedly intertextual, referring primarily to his other works and rarely to those of others. For instance, the poems "dread nay" and "Something there" (1974) cannot be approached without a knowledge of the world and art of Beckett's prose pieces since "Imagination Dead Imagine" (1965) like "Ping" (1967) and "Lessness" (1970). By creating such connections between his works Beckett hints at the existence of an implausible whole to his peculiar universe. In the poems "Roundelay" and "thither" (pub. 1976) repetition and variation / permutation and combination lead to slight differences in image and music bringing into play equally slight structures of exquisite free-floating symmetry. His last poems like "neither" (1979) and the three-poem sequence "PPS" create a gripping 'microverse' of the imagination in the effort to offer a metaphor for problematic metaphysical or aesthetic equations that beset him. They are vividly memorable and a paean to language's power to body forth the invisible and unnamable, in spite of Beckett's insistence that it just cannot be done. They may even have transcended the roots of resistance in language, those which Beckett had said he found impossible to transcend, as much as one is able to using language, according to the present writer.

In the beginning Beckett's poems were typical of the Zeitgeist that he began writing in. But in the end they areoriginal and meanwhile he has also spontaneously evolved into a leading representative of Post-modernism. Although "all strange away"[21] to the uninitiated reader, Beckett's poems; especially the finer ones, refuse to be forgotten or ignored and compel this exploration of their intricate secrets. (Endnotes)

Notes

1. John Calder, "An Introduction," *A Samuel Beckett Reader* ed. John Calder (London: Picador, 1983) 40.
2. Martin Esslin, "Samuel Beckett's Poems," *Beckett at Sixty: A Festschrift*, ed. John Calder (London: Calder & Boyars, 1967) 55.
3. The other art-movements referred to are, naturally, Unanimism, Symbolism, Dadaism, Expressionism, Futurism, the Aesthetic Decadence, Imagism, Vorticism, Verticalism etc. Among the leading poets of these movements were Pierre Jean Jouve, Paul Verlaine, Louis Aragon, Tristan Tzara, F.T. Marinetti, Stefan George, T.E. Hulme and Hans Arp.
4. Surreal: Having the intense irrationality of a dream. Surrealism: The principles, ideals or practice of producing fantastic or incongruous imagery or effects in art, literature, film or theater by means of unnatural juxtapositions or combinations. Surrealistic: Having ,a strange, dream-like atmosphere or quality like that of a surrealist painting. *Webster's 9th New Collegiate Dictionary* (Masachusetts:Merriam-Webster, 1988) 1188.
5. John Fletcher, "Beckett as Poet," *Samuel Beckett: A Collection of Critical Essays*, ed. Ruby Cohn (New York: McGraw - Hill, 1975) 41.

6. Marjorie Perloff, *The Poetics of Indeterminacy: Rimbaud to Cage*, (New Jersey, Princeton U.P., 1981)
7. John Pilling, *Samuel Beckett*, (London: Routledge & Kegan Paul, 1976)
8. Lawrence E. Harvey, *Samuel Beckett: Poet & Critic* (New Jersey, Princeton U.P./ 1970) 273.
9. David Hayman, "Beckett: Impoverishing the Means/Empowering the Matter," *Beckett Translating/ Translating Beckett*, ed. A.W. Friedman et al (London: Pennsylvania U.P., 1986) 111.
10. Hayman 112.
11. Samuel Beckett, in Harvey's *Samuel Beckett* 272.
12. Hugh Kenner, *A Reader's Guide to Samuel Beckett*, (London: Thames & Hudson, 1973) 42.
13. Kenner 45.
14. Beckett, "Moerike on Mozart," *Disjecta*, ed. Ruby Cohn (London: Calder, 1984) 61.
15. Israel Shenker, "An Interview with Samuel Beckett," *Samuel Beckett: The Critical Heritage*, ed. Lawrence Graver & Raymond Federman (London: Routledge & Kegan Paul 1979)
16. Esslin, "Samuel Beckett's Poems," *Beckett at Sixty* 59. This quote has been expanded slightly for clarity.
17. Minimalism: A style or technique (as in music or design) that is characterized by the use of few and simple elements. Minimal art: Abstract art consisting primarily of simple geometric forms executed in an impersonal style. (Related words; Minimal, minimalist, minimalistic) *Webster's Dictionary* 756.
18. Mannerism: An art style in late 16th century Europe characterised by spatial incongruity and excessive elongation of the human figures. ARTIFICIALITY. PRECIOSITY. An exaggerated or affected adherence to a particular style or manner. *Webster's* 724.
19. By John Barth, the famous American novelist who wrote the novels *The Sot-Weed Factor, Giles Goat-boy* etc.
20. *Rethinking Beckett* eds. Lance St. John Butler & Robin J. Davies (London: Macmillan, 1990)
21. Beckett, *Collected Shorter Prose 1945-'80*, (London: Calder, 1986) 117.

1

The Early Phase: The Years of Learning

Beckett began his career as a poet by writing poems that were published in small literary magazines like *Transition*, edited by sensitive art-purveyors like Eugene Jolas who viewed the avant-garde favourably. He was only in his twenties. But his poems reveal an exceptional intelligence at work. Joyce respected him. Beckett called his early poems, published here and there, the jettisoned poems. He did not think much of them. This is evident from the fact that of the poems published during 1929 to 1934 he allowed only "Whoroscope," "Home Olga" (1932) and "Gnome" to be reprinted in *Collected Poems 1930-'78*. The opinion of critics on his juvenilia is generally the same as his.

Excluding the three poems just mentioned, the others in English belonging to this period in the chronological order of their appearance are "For Future Reference (Reality and Beyond)" (1930), "From the Only Poet to a Shining Whore" (1930), "Hell Crane to Starling," "Casket of Pralinen to a Daughter of a Dissipated Mandarin," "Text," "Yoke of Liberty," "Return to the Vestry" (all pub. 1931), a sonnet (the second version) in the short story "Sedendo et Quiescendo" (1932) and "Calvary by Night" (the second version) in "A Wet Night," a short story in the collection *More Pricks Than Kicks* (1934). The early versions of the sonnet and "Calvary by Night" are found in *Dream of Fair to Middling Women*, Beckett's incomplete prose novel that he abandoned by 1932 that was published posthumously. *Dream* also contains his first attempt at writing verse in French.

As far as one knows the jettisoned poems have not been reprinted. But they are made available to the reader in Harvey's book. Harvey mentions that Beckett wrote two other sonnets. They were probably to, for and on Peggy Sinclair. Some of his poems (e.g., the sonnet) and characters, especially Belacqua Shuah's sweet-heart Smeraldina-Rima (little emerald rhyme) in *Dream* and *MPTK*, are based on her. Beckett's bibliographers Federman and Fletcher list a handwritten sonnet on the back of a manuscript of "Whoroscope" that is kept at the University of Texas library. There is confusion as to whether this sonnet is one of those mentioned by Harvey or not. Not having been published as yet, as far as one knows, these sonnets cannot be discussed. What can be studied are the twelve poems mentioned so far.

1929-'34 was also the period in which Beckett was writing and honing the thirteen poems that went into the making of *Echo's Bones*, his first collection of poems. The first version of "Alba" was published in 1931. Beckett translated Eugene Montale's "Delta" from the Italian in 1930. Ernst Moerman's "Louis Armstrong," Rimbaud's "Le Bateau Ivre" (The Drunken Boat) and poems by the famous Surrealists Eluard, René Crevel and André Breton were also ones he translated from the French in these years. It can be deduced from all this activity that Beckett's initial inclination was indeed towards poetry.

"For Future Reference" was Beckett's first published poem. It originally appeared under the presumptuous title of "Reality and Beyond." It was written, as a reference in line fifty-nine to Giordano Bruno indicates, in roughly the same frame of mind as his essay "Dante. . . Bruno.Vico..Joyce." The essay has become justly famous. The poem, on the other hand, is a failure.

The poem is ostensibly about the fear of teachers and heights. Some of its features are noteworthy. It is written in free verse that ranges too close to prose cut into lines for the reader to feel that Beckett would ever make a mark on prosody. He did not. But in the second half of the first stanza he yokes sound and sense together onomatopoeically in a manner reminiscent of Browning's and Hopkins's, suggesting in embryo certain achievements of his in some of his later, more memorable poems in *Echo's Bones* etc. In them he captures the rhythms of actions and verbs like walking, cycling and sailing in words, the meanings of which only serve to reinforce the effect of equivalence. In Browning's "Rabbi Ben Ezra" one finds the effective line:" Irks care the crop-full bird? Frets doubt the maw-crammed beast?"[1] (Stanza IV, 1. 6). The full crop of the bird and the crammed maw of the beast are made evident to the reader's ear by the use of many consonantal stops. In Hopkins's "The Wreck of the Deutschland" the storm's description reads:

> And the sea flint flake, black-backed in the regular blow,
> Sitting East northeast, in cursed quarter, the wiry and white-
> fiery and whirlwind-swivellèd snow
> Spins to the widow-making unchilding unfathering deeps.[2]
> (Stanza 13, 1. 4-8)

One can hear the sea rage in these lines. In both these examples ingenuity is at work. They depend on the arrayal of harsh clusters of consonants, jaw-breaking to pronounce, to convey the sense. Sensitivity to the possibilities of alliteration, consonance, assonance, euphony, cacophony and onomatopoeia is exploited. Joyce, Shakespeare and Dickens, as Beckett points out in his seminal essay of 1929 on the former, were capable of using these techniques to the full in their works.[3] In his verse, Beckett tried to employ this difficult approach but succeeded only fitfully. However in "For Future Reference," a poem of seventy-eight lines, such a moment does occur.

> But I stilled my cringing
> and smote him
> yes oh my strength !
> smashed
> mashed (peace my incisors !)
> flayed and crushed him
> with a ready are you steady
> cuff-discharge.
> But did I ?[4] (1. 11-20)

The consonantal play evokes the sound of a brawl convincingly.

Except for a few exonerating points like this "For Future Reference" is, generally speaking, unclear in some of its parts and affected in its thrust for originality. The best part of the poem is the image in the penultimate lines: "So the snowy floor of the parrot's cell/burning at dawn."[5] (1. 76, 77). It is possible to explain these lines by stating that "parrot" is a metaphor for 'student.' It is not the meaning but the striking dream-like beauty of the image that actually appeals. Something elusive in it escapes the grasp of the reader who tries to gauge the cause, receding and giving the lines their aesthetically valuable dimension. "For Future Reference" was written in 1929 and published in 1930. "Whoroscope," Beckett's next venture into poetry, was both written and published in 1930. It shows a marked improvement in Beckett's poetic ability. It is the only poem written by Beckett that has received much attention. The Cartesian connection is responsible for this. What impresses one reading it many years after its genesis is no longer its alleged obscurity or imitativeness. These have been cleared up and accounted for by the critics. It is the writer's daring in attempting the nuances possible to the stream-of-consciousness technique — to reveal intelligently the intricate manner of the working of the mind and the artist simulating this phenomenon — in the medium of 'verse' that is remarkable. Beckett does it almost as effectively as it has been done in prose by writers like Joyce.

The associative nature of "Whoroscope" gives it poetic grace. What one means by the word 'associative' here is the architectonics peculiar to this poem by which its lines are not only connected but unfold. It has an internal logic linking sound to sound, image and image, meaning to meaning, allusion to allusion etc., that forms an absorbing pattern that the reader has to discover. These 'touches' that cause the contact between the lines of the poem have to be verbalized for their beauty to be realized.

The image of the egg that appears first in the second line of the poem, for example, is the leitmotif that keeps surfacing in the flow of Beckett's Descartes' thoughts and memories. It is, in other words, the thread or symbol that unites the poem's disparate stanzas. As the notes to the poem put it succinctly and poetically "the shuttle of a ripening egg combs the warp of his days."[6] This is an interesting example of how a word that is also a sign can act in a manner that helps the unifying process in an associative poem. Here it gives the poem's lines their authentic cognizable semblance of belonging to a single consciousness.

Another type of association it is possible to notice in the poem is that based on assonance and consonance. The last line of the first stanza reads "Give it to Gillot."[7] The first word of the second stanza is "Galileo."[8] The reader may be non-plussed for a moment, unable to find the reason for Descartes to suddenly remember Galileo. But he will quickly latch on to the fact that the memory is suggested to him partly by the phonemes of his earlier thought. In revealing the role played by the mind's tendency to echo sounds in its patterning of thoughts Beckett hints at how random leaps of thought may not be as arbitrary as they seem. By bringing processes like this to light, and creating such connections in the poem, he also shows the artist's method of operation. His is a highly sensitive endeavour like that of the mind in its complexity and makes use of both the conscious and the unconscious. This is especially so with regard to any experiment with the presentation of the 'pre-speech' level of the consciousness in poems like "Whoroscope."

Just as sounds in series and the echoic tendency of minds and poets can build up a connected edifice of lines, the use of words and meanings can also lead a poem on by creating associations that make clear the reasons for the lines that precede or follow. The sixth stanza of "Whoroscope" is a typically deft example. The stanza reads:

> My squinty doaty !
> I hid and you sook.
> And Francine my precious fruit of a house-and-parlour foetus!
> What an exfoliation!
> Her little grey-flayed epidermis and scarlet tonsils!
> My one child
> scourged by a fever to stagnant murky blood.
> blood!
> Oh Harvey beloved
> how shall the red and white, the many in the few
> (dear bloodswirling Harvey)
> eddy through that cracked beater?
> And the fourth Henry came to the crypt of the arrow.[9] (1. 29-41)

The notes given by Beckett tell us that lines twenty-nine and thirty refer to the fact that "as a child [Descartes] played with a little cross-eyed girl."[10] The lines that follow (1. 31-36) are explained by the notes as referring to "his daughter [who] died of scarlet fever at the age of six"[11] As Harvey says, "the recollection of one beloved child brings another to mind."[12] He next points out how "the word 'blood' (1. 36) forms a transition to the next part of the poem, where the narrator's thoughts turn to the circulation of blood and its discoverer, William Harvey (1. 37-40)."[13] In line forty "cracked beater" is, among other things, a metaphor for 'heart' and 'dying.' This gives rise to DesCartes' next memory, encapsulated in line forty-one and explained in the notes as: "the heart of Henry IV was received at the Jesuit College of La Fleche while Des Cartes was still a student there."[14] The stanza is thus a well-knit unit that links memory to memory (child → child), word to idea (blood → circulation) and meaning to hidden allusion (heart → death) to form a coherent complicated web of thoughts. It is a tribute to the unconscious, revealing that it has a rigorous logic all its own. It is also one to the art of poetry where this logic may be duplicated and explored. In instances like this Beckett is seen to be a fine poet, capable of rivalling his peers James Joyce, T.S. Eliot and Ezra Pound who too have such sections in their works *Ulysses*, *The Waste Land* and *The Cantos*.

Association also occurs in "Whoroscope" at the wider level of echoes, allusions and references. As in Eliot's *The Waste Land* intertextuality and referentiality that may be geographic, historical, theological, multi-lingual, metaphoric, aesthetic etc., situate the poem in a labyrinth where it becomes in its sections or parts signifiers that are irreducible and constantly defer meaning. The resultant play of contexts, the spectres of which are thrown up by Beckett's use of allusiveness as a conscious literary technique, leads to the poem being a powerful 'structural' entity. Associativeness, it can be understood, works not only as an internal organizing principle as it did in the examples cited so far but also as a means whereby the text may point away from itself to others to reinforce its literary strength structurally and semantically. To illustrate this an analysis of the eleventh stanza of the poem helps:

> Anna Maria !
> She reads Moses and says her love is crucified.[15]
> Leider ! Leider ! she bloomed and withered
> a pale abusive parakeet in a mainstreet window."[16]

The notes inform us that Anna Maria Schumann was a "Dutchblue-stocking, a pious pupil of Voët, the adversary of DesCartes."[17] The stanza fits into the poem neatly, both biographically and because lines forty-five to eighty-three are about DesCartes' spiritual, religious and theological speculations. Intertextually, the stanza refers to Beckett's source for the details of DesCartes' life, Adrien Baillet's *La Vie de Monsieur DesCartes* (The life of Mr. DesCartes). The references in the stanza are explicitly to Miss. Schumann and Moses and implicitly to St. Ignatius of Loyola and Jesus Christ. The stanza's narrator, the annotator of the poem, Beckett and DesCartes are also implicated. Intertextuality and referentiality combine hereto link periods of history, different books, people, disciplines, languages, places and events to suggest the palpable continuum of life via the fragments of art. What is of interest here is not the truth of the poet's utterance. As a matter of fact Beckett's and DesCartes' views, like Baillet's, on Miss Schumann are biased.[18] But Beckett's ability to make all that he writes necessary using the principle of associativeness is impressive. In this context "Whoroscope" has a tendency to longevity owing to its compressed reconditeness that is its chief virtue. It remains an important experiment among Beckett's works, indicating the inherent tendency of language to cohere, forming structural relationships between its units. This happens in the mind of the careful reader. "Whoroscope" is also important as a poem that becomes unified on a premise that is not metrical or thematic as is usual, but in its exploitation of the structure of the psyche and its operation as a suitable 'form' for poetry.

In 1930, besides "For Future Reference" and "Whoroscope", the poem "From the Only Poet to a Shining Whore" was also published. The ambience of the poem is Dantescan. The influence of the Bible is clear. The ironical tone is Beckett's. The poem is worth quoting fully.

> Rahab of the holy battlements,
> bright dripping shaft
> in the bright bright patient
> pearl-brow dawn-dusk lover of the sun.
> Puttanina mia !
> You hid them happy in the high flax,
> pale before the fords
> of Jordan, and the red waters
> and you lowered a pledge of scarlet hemp.
>
> Oh radiant, oh angry, oh Beatrice
> she foul with the victory
> of the bloodless fingers
> and proud, and you, Beatrice, mother, sister, daughter, belovèd
> fierce pale flame
> of doubt, and God's sorrow
> and my sorrow.[19]

The "Only Poet" is Dante. That Beckett called him thus speaks volumes about his admiration of Dante's mastery over the art of poetry. Dante's is the mask or persona from which these arresting lines of verse issue. "The Shining Whore" to whom the poem is dedicated, who is addressed in the title and the first stanza, is Rahab. The references are to the book of *Joshua* in the Old Testament and Dante's *Paradiso*. The Bible explains that Rahab, though a harlot, was saved because her faith in the only true and living God led her to preserve the lives of two of his people. She became an example of trust, of the fear of the Lord, of hope in His mercy, charity, good works and obedience. She was granted not only her salvation but that of her family. She was also given the grace of being the only Canaanite from whom God's curse was removed in the Old Testament, allowed to marry into the godly line of Abraham's descendants. She is one of the ancestors of King David and the Messiah Jesus Christ. She is an emblem of God's impartiality and the power of His grace. The Cantos in *Paradiso* from which Beckett drew his inspiration are the third and the ninth. Rahab's glory is shown in the metaphors Beckett substitutes for her. The first, that of the "bright dripping shaft," was probably inspired by Dante's line in Canto IX of *Paradiso* about the glory of heavenly souls. He writes that they shine like "the sun's rays glitter[ing] on water clear."[20] The second and third metaphors, put in Hopkinsian compounds, substitute a "pearl" and the planet of Venus for her. It may be because she was one of those whose love was initially too much of the earth, i.e., sensual, that the latter metaphor is used. To illustrate her humanness by comparison, the metaphors are made against the background of God's greater glory that is suggested by the image of the "sun." The second part of the stanza stresses felicitously on the words "happy" and "pale" since these adjectives include the fear and 'wonder' of both Rahab and Joshua's soldier-spies whom she helped in Jericho, regarding God's power as shown in His miracles of the parting of the Red Sea and Jordan. The second half of the first stanza retells the episode involving Rahab recorded in the second and third chapters of *Joshua.*

The first section of the poem, pietistic in content in the mould of its originals, differs in spirit from the second. In the latter half of the poem Beckett emerges from behind the mask of Dante partly. Beatrice is introduced and a second look is taken at Rahab. Unsatisfying conclusions are drawn about their natures.

Unlike Dante's Beatrice, Beckett's is not only "radiant" but also "angry" and a "fierce pale flame / of doubt," a cause of "sorrow" to the narrator and God. And Rahab becomes not only a victor but also "foul" and "proud." The difference in perception reveals the gap between Beckett and his mentors, in this case the authors of *Joshua* and *Paradiso*. His vision has little or no place in it for the virtue displayed by these ancient masters in their ability to portray redeemed or ideal characters like Rahab and Beatrice. This twist in the view-point, slightly obscured by the tricky use of pronouns like "you" and "she" in the poem, brings one back to the title. The realisation dawns that the "Only Poet" could also be Beckett and that "the Shining Whore" is a symbol of his preference for a sinful life with the possibility of change somewhere along the way to the consistently saintly life typified by the fictionalized Beatrice. At a deeper level he rejects both these types of humanity, affirming instead the dedication that makes 'fine' art like Dante's possible. The dilemma of facing serious issues like salvation is thus deferred in Beckett's works, although thought deeply about, and Art is exalted at the expense of the divine.

In 1931 Edward Titus, the editor of *The European Caravan*, published in it four new Beckett poems. The first, titled "Hell Crane to Starling," refers to Canto V of Dante's *Inferno* where the souls of those damned for the sins of incontinence are compared to cranes and starlings. The allusions in the poem are to *Genesis* and *Ezekiel*. The poem deals with the conflict in a young man's mind between the desire to seduce a woman and the knowledge that it is wrong. The conflict is not resolved but the carpe diem note sounds out more strongly than the puritanical one. Much of the complexity of the poem is a result of the young Beckett's mistaken impression that obscure difficult poetry written for its own sake is important. "Hell Crane" is not one of Beckett's better poems.

The second poem in the series was "Casket of Pralinen for a Daughter of a Dissipated Mandarin." "Hell Crane" can be considered as a poem on the need to balance the opposed drives in the self between eroticism and chastity. "Casket of Pralinen. . . " is about the tensions between Beauty (typified by woman and sex), Art (particularised by idealised notions of feminine mystique) and Truth (signified by God, Christ and the problem of the existence of suffering and mercy simultaneously in the world). In the course of the poem riddled by faults in style that emanate from Joycean and Browningesque sections and a subjectivity unleashed to the point of immaturity in the choice of personal and obscure references one section is scintillating. It stretches from the twenty-seventh to the forty-fifth line.

> What is this that is more
> than the anguish of Beauty,
> this gale of pain that was not prepared
> in the caves of her eyes ?
>
> Is it enough
> a stitch in the hem of the garment of God ?
>
> To-night her gaze would be less
> than a lark's barred sunlight.
>
> Oh I am ashamed
> of all clumsy artistry
> I am ashamed of trying
> to arrange words
> of everything but the ingenuous fibres
> that suffer honestly.
>
> Fool ! do you hope to untangle
> the knot of God's pain ?

Melancholy Christ that was a soft one !
Oh yes I think that was perhaps just a very little inclined to be
rather too self-conscious.[21]

The passage indicates what Beckett may have achieved if he had nurtured in himself the pietistic and beauty-oriented tendencies of Continental masters like Dante. The reference in the thirty-second line in this "dialogue of self and soul"[22] is to the incident recorded in Luke 8.43-48 where a woman who believes that if she could just touch the hem of Jesus's robe she would instantly be healed is shown. She recovers, naturally, and He commends her faith. In the context of the poem Beckett sways between wanting to be a Christian, a lover and an artist. His insight tells him he can travel on only one of these roads. But the poem is a witness to his delaying, doubts, hesitations and the fact that out of this struggle concerning important issues and choices a self-reflexive art can be made. Even as he discusses abiding themes like woman, sex, love, suffering, God, salvation, beauty, the finiteness of human understanding etc., he is aware that a poet's over-riding concern is with language. To allow this knowledge into the open in his verse is a trait that foreshadows Post-modernism. In using critical self-reflexivity as a technique Beckett is certainly one of the initiators of what one can only call 'metaverse,' for want of a better term. Metaverse, when refined, leads to powerful poems like Ted Hughes's "Thought-Fox" where the act of writing and what is written is integrated into a piece that also reveals an 'illusion' of how it has been made. In Hughes's poem lines like "And this blank page where the fingers move" and "The page is printed"[23] are the result. Metaverse can be thought of as a parallel to the post-modern forms of metafiction and metatheatre.

The third in the series of poems that was published in The European Caravan was "Text." Much that was said of "Casket of Pralinen . . . " is applicable to "Text" also. It is long and highly allusive with the lines having Beckettian fictionalized speakers as diverse as the Marcel of Proust's *A la Recherche du Temps Perdu* (*Remembrance of Things Past*), the Tiresias of myth and Dante's *Inferno*, Job, Boccaccio, figures from Dante's gallery of the picturesque damned and Dante's Virgil. The poem never comes to rest as complicated themes that include the nature of gender, human\sympathy, divine power, mercy, suffering, art's immortality etc., jostle in it. The poem makes little sense to a reader who cannot apply Harvey's book to it as a concordance. But impressive passages in it make it an interesting venture, albeit loose, in the mode of Modernism. In places, Browning's style is carried off with ease. Pound was influenced by that style's poetic vigour as can be seen from poems like "Near Perigord." Beckett too imitates and catches it. Thus in "Text" when Job addresses God the verse is serious, reminding one of the gravity of the Authorised King James Version of the Bible as well as Browning's ability to recreate its sublimity in verse in poems like "Saul." The scepticism is Beckett's contribution. One can compare a stanza of Browning's from "Rabbi Ben Ezra" with Beckett's imitation in "Text" to clarify what is meant.

> So take and use Thy work:
> Amend what flaws may lurk,
> What strain o' the stuff what warpings past the aim!
> My times be in Thy hand !
> Perfect the cup as planned !
> Let age approve of youth, and death complete the same ![2]
> ("Rabbi Ben Ezra", last stanza)

> Open Thou my lips and
> (if one dare make a suggestion)
> Thine eye of skyflesh.
> Am I a token of Godcraft ?
> The masterpiece of a scourged apprentice?[25]
> ("Text", 1. 20-25)

"Text" has several other memorable passages like this but the heavily allusive sections in it disrupt the poem's decorum.

"Yoke of Liberty," the last in the series, stands in contrast to all the Beckettian poems looked at so far. It is bereft of allusions, references and echoes. Beckett has borrowed the title from Dante but in the context of the poem this ceases to be important. "Yoke of Liberty" is Beckett's first lyric. That part of M.H. Abram's definition of the lyric that it is ". . . a brief expression of a mood or state of feeling"[26] may be relevant here.

YOKE OF LIBERTY

The lips of her desire are grey
and parted like a silk loop
threatening
a slight wanton wound.
She preys wearily
on sensitive wild things
proud to be torn
by the grave crouch of her beauty.
But she will die and her snare tendered so patiently
to my tamed watchful sorrow
will break and hang
in a pitiful crescent.[27]

Pedantry finds little place in this poem that hardly falters. In its emotional tone it brings to mind some of Byron's incomparable love lyrics like "When we two parted" and "She walks in beauty like the night."[28] The sexual imagery of the first section where the words "lips," "grey" and "slight" are all loaded invokes, along with the second section, the literary archetype of the 'femme fatale' who is aged, adulterous and a dangerous influence on the young. But the third section reveals the artist's distance from his experiences, however risky they may be to him at a moral level, and humanizes the nameless woman of the poem by bringing to the reader's notice the fact that she will die. The word "tamed" in the latter part of the poem is ambiguous. Does it mean the poet fell to the woman's wiles or resisted her successfully? In the light of the content of the poem the title takes on added significance. Beckett, it suggests, refuses to substitute the worship of art for the worship of woman. But he is aware that the liberty he chooses is as much of a prison, the only difference being that it is his choice and hence bearable. The poem deals with the same theme as Henry James's novel The Ambassadors and T.S Eliot's poem "Portrait of a Lady." In its small way it almost attains the same excellence.

The last of Beckett's poems to be published in 1931 was "Return to the Vestry." It appeared in *The New Review: An International Notebook for the Arts*. It relates the story of Beckett's visit to the grave of Pierre de Ronsard, one of France's great poets of the past, and his consequent thoughts. One could call it a modern elegy. Since it is a tribute to Ronsard echoes of a poem of his occur frequently in it. Ronsard was a priest by profession and made a pilgrimage that he described in his ode "Magie, ou deliverance d'amour" (Magic, or deliverance from love). Beckett's poem, Harvey notes, parodies the purification rites performed by Ronsard then that are described in the French poem[29] but also expresses genuine sorrow over his death and the fate of his poetry which is nearly forgotten. The last section of the poem, addressed to Anteros who was a god against life and love, is disturbing.

Gentle Anteros
dark and dispassionate
come a grave snake with peace to my quarry
and choke my regret
noble Anteros
and coil at the door of my quarry tomb
and span its rim with a luminous awning
shallow and dim

as a grey tilt of silk filtering sadly
the weary triumph of morning.
Or mock a duller impurity.[30] (1.35-46)

The lines seem to come from a willing denizen of infernal regions. The appearance of the words "gentle," "peace," "noble," "luminous" and "triumph" in these lines clashes with "dark," "dispassionate," "grave," "choke" etc. This gives the stanza its contradictory air where positive tensions counter the generally chilling drift of the lines, making them effective.

Beckett's *Dream* contains a sonnet from its protagonist Belacqua Shuah to the Smeraldina Rima. Shuah is Beckett's fictional alter-ego, as the inverted capital letters of his name in which S.B becomes B.S suggest. The sonnet was inspired presumably by Beckett's reading of J.A. Symonds's translation of Michaelangelo's Italian sonnets.[31]

At last I find in my confused soul
Dark with the dark flame of the cypresses
The certitude that I cannot be whole
Consummate, finally achieved, unless

I be consumed and fused in the white heat
Of her sad finite essence, so that none
Shall sever us who are at last complete
Eternally, irrevocably one,

One with the birdless, cloudless, colourless skies
One with the bright purity of the fire
Of which we are and for which we must die
A rapturous strange death and be entire.

Like syzygetic stars, supernly bright
Conjoined in One and in the Infinite ![32]

A simpler version of the sonnet appears in "Sedendo et Quiescendo." The sonnet does not flow smoothly. Line thirteen is the only memorable one. One feels that the whole exercise is inflated hyperbole unnecessarily masquerading as quasi-mystical experience to disguise the actual emotion that is only sexual desire inspired and inflated by the lascivious little god, Priapus. John Pilling, considering the poem as an experiment in traditional metrics, says that "the occasional infelicities of phrase and rhythm seem deliberate, yet there is a fatigue in rhyme and scansion that suggests no formal mode would ever have suited Beckett."[33] What Beckett said of the sonnet as a form once may be applicable here. Commenting on sonneteers in "Recent Irish Poetry" (1934) he notes: "What is badly needed at the present moment is some small Malherbe of free verse to sit on the sonnet and put it out of action for two hundred years at least."[34]

"Home Olga," Beckett's tongue-in-cheek tribute to Joyce, was published in 1932. Its form is that of the acrostic. The first letters of the ten lines of verse in the poem spell out the name James Joyce. Richard Ellmann, Joyce's biographer, makes the title out to be a defamiliarisation of "homo-logos," i.e., "man-word,"[35] suggesting that it is a compliment to Joyce's Christ-like genius with language. Harvey is of the opinion that the title implies Beckett's decision to get off the "Joyce-bandwagon."[36] Both the readings are plausible. Beckett did stop imitating Joyce and find his style but it took him several years. As a poem, "Home Olga" is of little interest except to Joyceans and Beckettians. It contains one good line on the mythical Daedalus that goes: "Swoops and loops of love and silence in the eye of the sun and view of the mew."[37]

Beckett did not publish any new poems in 1933. But in the next year both "Gnome" and "Calvary by Night" appeared. "Gnome," though only a quatrain, requires much attention.

Spend the years of learning squandering
Courage for the years of wandering
Through a world, politely turning
From the loutishness of learning.[38]

Beckett has said that "Gnome" was inspired by Goethe's 'xenien.' The embryo of "Gnome" can be seen in "For Future Reference." It shows the same distaste for education.

Gnome means maxim or aphorism. In the Greek it means opinion. Paradigmatically the title brings to mind the words gnomic, gnostic and gnosis. The word itself derives its existence from the Greek gignoskein which means 'to know.'[39] The title of the poem alludes to the poem's literary lineage. A xenien is terse like an epigram. It also meant a gift given by a host to guests as an act of hospitality in ancient Greece. The English word 'xenial' refers to this extinct practice. Goethe borrowed the form and used it in German. It is possible to consider "Gnome" as a gift of advice to the reader and the sole example in English of another revival and adaptation of the form, this time from the German. The choice reveals Beckett's penchant for the exotic. Plumbing for the unknown meaning of the word 'gnome' is a similar act.

This is again one of the few poems written by Beckett in English that makes use of sustained metre, the regular stanza and end-rhymes. The absence of punctuation works as a trick that seems to prise the text open into plurality but actually simplifies it. The poem presents personal experience in the guise of generalisation.

The third line in the poem is rich in layers. The world turns, not only on its axis and in its orbit but also away from the absent 'I' in the poem. It exhibits a dislike for pedantry. The reader of the poem turns, while reading it, away from "the loutishness of learning." The absent self in the poem also turns away from what was irrelevant in his past. The use of the indefinite article in "a world" suggests that the world in question is more an internal one than the objective circumstances surrounding the narrative voice. If one allows for the possibility of gaps and ellipsis in the poem the meaning becomes indeterminate and multiple possibilities may occur to the reader.

"Gnome" has an interesting autobiographical context. After resigning from his post as an instructor at Trinity College, Dublin, in 1931 to become a writer Beckett spent the next few years wandering uncertainly in France, Germany, Ireland and England. This is its background.

"Gnome" is Cartesian. The shadow of DesCartes and his system looms behind it. DesCartes would have agreed with Beckett that learning is no substitute for "courage." But one doubts if he would have thought of his courage as having been squandered by learning. Beckett is more radical. There is a deeper sense in which the poem is linked to DesCartes. The issues inherent in the poem are framed in the Cartesian mode, i.e., they are dualistic. Two of the important themes being examined are the relationship between the self and the world, a problematic dialectic in itself, and the nature of the subject as opposed to the world. A brief stating of the antinomies set against each other in the poem to create aesthetic tension may be worth introducing here.

The years of learning (Die Lehrjahre)	/	The years of wandering (Die Wanderjahre)[40]
Knowledge	/	Experience
Intellect	/	Emotion

The latter pairs are inferences. Beckett's sympathies are with the second set.

That the poem limits literary allusiveness to the minimum and eschews linguistic exhibitionism of the Joycean variety is not only predictive of Beckett's poems of his mature years but also in keeping with its anti-scholastic tone.

The last poem of the period under consideration, "Calvary by Night," is better in the truncated satiric form that is found in "A Wet Night" than it is in its first version. The atmosphere of the poem is lyrical. The influence of surrealists like Eluard can be sensed. The images of creation and coitus are introduced as metaphors in the poem. The typographic arrangement of the poem is such that the budding, blooming and withering of a flower is simulated by the length of the lines. The cyclical or spiral pattern is incorporated by the poem ending and beginning with the same images and words.

CALVARY BY NIGHT

the water
the waste of water
in the womb of water
an pansy leaps

rocket of bloom flare flower of night wilt for me
on the breasts of the water it has closed it has made
an act of floral presence in the water
the tranquil act of its cycle on the waste
from the spouting forth to the re-enwombing
untroubled bow of petalline sweet-smellingness
kingfisher abated
drowned for me
lamb of insustenance mine

till the clamour of a blue bloom
beat on the walls of the womb of
the waste of
the water[41]

The poem is about the act of creation and the fact that, according to Beckett, what is created is beautiful but ephemeral. Yet aesthetic creation is glorified. "Calvary by Night" looks backward to all the poems studied so far and forward to "The Vulture" where the same theme is again explored, minus the erotic note, more powerfully. In this poem the concerns of Beckett's jettisoned poems are reflected and summed up microcosmically. The attractiveness of Christianity and eroticism as ways of life and the knowledge that Art is the path Beckett wishes to walk on are the strands that are highlighted.

The presence of the many influences on Beckett like Dante, the Bible, DesCartes, Joyce etc., gives the jettisoned poems we have been looking at depth but hinder Beckett's attempt in his "years of learning" to find his own style. But gradually the allusions, references and echoes appear only where necessary and the Joycean language becomes more Beckettian. In sections in all the poems where this balance is struck the result is poetic. The best examples are found in "Text."

Eliot resurrected Dante's poetic power briefly in sections of "Ash Wednesday." For example, in Section II, one comes across these lines:

> Lady, three white leopards sat under a juniper-tree
> In the cool of the day, having fed to satiety
> On my legs my heart my liver and that which had been
>   contained
> In the hollow round of my skull. . .[42] (1. 1-4 a)

Beckett too literally resurrects it in brief segments like the one given below in "Text." The frame is again Biblical, as it often was in his early poems.

Worms breed in their red tears
as they slouch by unnamed
scorned by the black ferry
despairing of death
who shall not scour in swift joy
the bright hill's girdle
nor tremble with the dark pride of torture
and the bitter indignity of an ingenious damnation.
Lo-Ruhama Lo-Ruhama
Pity is quick with death.[43] (1. 54-63)

Such sections make the jettisoned poems alluring, except when compared with the authenticity of some of Beckett's mature poems in his original style. The main difference seems to be that Beckett's better poems, unlike these, excel on the whole and not just in occasional patches.

Notes and References

1. Robert Browning, "Rabbi Ben Ezra," *The Golden Treasury of English Songs and Lyrics* ed. F.T. Palgrave (London: Dent, 1955) 364.
2. G.M. Hopkins, "The Wreck of the Deutschland," *The Faber Book of Modern Verse* eds. Michael Roberts, Peter Porter (London: Faber, 1982) 57.
3. Samuel Beckett, "Dante ... Bruno . Vico .. Joyce," *Disjecta* ed. Ruby Cohn (London: Calder, 1984) 28.
4. Beckett, "-For Future Reference," in Harvey's *Samuel Beckett* (New Jersey: Princeton U.P., 1970) 299.
5. Ibid., 301.
6. Beckett, "Whoroscope / Notes," *Collected Poems 1930-1978* (London: Calder, 1984) 5.
7. Ibid., 1.
8. Ibid.
9. Ibid., 2.
10. Ibid., 5.
11. Ibid.
12. Lawrence E. Harvey, *Samuel Beckett. Poet & Critic* (New Jersey: Princeton U.P., 1970) 20.

13. Ibid., 21.
14. Beckett "Whoroscope/Notes," *C.P.* 5.
15. In Adrien Baillet's *La Vie de Monsieur DesCartes* (1691), he writes of Anna Maria Schurmann as one who had "taken for her motto the beautiful saying of the martyr, St. Ignatius, ["] Amor meus crucifix est ["]. The translation into English is by Harvey. The Latin means 'my love is crucified.' Beckett is referring to this section of Baillet's in line 69 of the poem. Harvey's translation makes the allusion clear to the reader. In Harvey 29.
16. Beckett, "Whoroscope / Notes," *C.P.* 3.
17. Ibid., 6.
18. In E.H. Broadbent's *The Pilgrim Church* the author comments on Miss. Schumann's life as exemplary throughout.
19. Beckett, "From the Only Poet to a Shining Whore," Harvey 306-7.
20. Dante, "Paradiso," *The Selected Works* trans. Lawrence Binyon, ed. Paolo Milano (London: Chatto & Windus, 1972) 414.
21. Beckett, "Casket of Pralinen for a Daughter of a Dissipated Mandarin," in Harvey 280-81.
22. W.B. Yeats, "A Dialogue of Self and Soul," *The Faber Book of Modern Verse* 77.
23. Ted Hughes, "The Thought-Fox," *The Faber Book of Modern Verse* 385.
24. Robert Browning, "Rabbi Ben Ezra," *Fifteen Poets* (Calcutta: O.U.P., 1985) 438.
25. Beckett, "Text," in Harvey 289.
26. M.H. Abrams, *A Glossary of Literary Terms* (India: Macmillan, 1978) 89.
27. Beckett, "Yoke of Liberty," in Harvey 314.
28. George Gordon Byron, *Fifteen Poets* 297-98.
29. I have not read this poem's translation or original. But the commentary on both Ronsard's and Beckett's poems are found in Harvey 308-312. This is my source.
30. Beckett, "Return to The Vestry," in Harvey 311-12.
31. John Pilling, *Samuel Beckett* (London: Routledge & Kegan Paul, 1976) 163.
32. Beckett, "At last I find in my confused soul," in Harvey 284.
33. Pilling, *Beckett* 163.
34. Beckett, "Recent Irish Poetry," *Disjecta* 74.
35. Richard Ellmann, *James Joyce* (London: O.U.P., 1966) 714 (paperback).

36. Harvey, *Beckett* 296.
37. Ibid., 297.
38. Beckett, "Gnome," *C.P.* 7.
39. Harvey, *Beckett* 221.
40. Ibid.
41. Beckett, "A Wet Night," *More Pricks Than Kicks* (London: Calder and Boyars, 1970) 65.
42. T.S. Eliot, *Selected Poems* (London: Faber, 1982) 85.
43. Beckett, "Text," in Harvey 295.

2

The Early Phase: The Years of Wandering

Echo's Bones, Beckett's first collection of poems, was initially titled "Echo's Bones and Other Precipitates." It contains thirteen poems. Beckett had triskaidekophilia. *Echo's Bones* is a "modern poetic sequence."[1] It appeared after poems like *The Waste Land* had become a common feature of the literary scene. Readers may have found it difficult, although new reading techniques were rapidly being evolved to cope with such challenging literature. The reactions to the poems were mainly negative. Richard Coe and Donald Davie refused to praise it. The poems rely on 'referents' and allusions unavailable to the reader and hence look impenetrable. But they can be made to yield their secrets and it becomes clear that many are ambitious failures. Some of them are powerful. Even the weak ones have a reason for their existence when considered as a part of the sequence where they mesh with the others like links in a chain. They also justify themselves by having lines, images or passages in them that are remarkable.

The poems were arranged for effect and not according to the chronology of their composition. The first poem, "The Vulture," is too mature to have been written before 1934. "Alba," on the other hand, was written in 1931. But it is placed fourth in the series. It appears in the collection in a modified version. "The Vulture," placed at the beginning of the cycle, sets the tone of the collection. It is like a prelude or an overture. The dominant chord struck, that of negation, was predictive of not only what followed in *Echo's Bones* but also of the mood of most of Beckett's major works like his famous 'Trilogy'. The other poems are lists, complaints, dawn-songs, prosaic travelogue-narratives, serenades, elegies and laments. The main themes include the ones already met with in Beckett's jettisoned poems, i.e., love, sex, women, art, God, Christ etc. The new important themes are many. The main ones are solitude, rejection, the family, change, death, exile etc., in keeping with the existential, nihilistic temper of the age in which Beckett was writing. Throughout, connections exist between Beckett's prose works *Dream* and *MPTK* and the poems. The vast storehouse of literature was freely tapped by Beckett. The major influences, as already stated in the introduction, included Ovid, Goethe, Rimbaud, Provençal verse-forms, Schopenhauer, Democritus and Walther von der Vogelweide, not to mention Beckett's perennial favourites like the Bible, Dante, DesCartes and Joyce. Lesser influences like Eliot, Browning and the others are too many to be completely listed. The language is a cross between the Joycean and the Beckettian. In the shorter poems Beckett's individuality begins to manifest itself. The last poem, "Echo's Bones," acts as an epilogue. It puts an end to the turbulent cathartic baring of the soul by the autodiegetic protagonist of the poems and announces Beckett's love of Death. It can be thought of as a summary of the collection's content.

A modern poetic sequence can be defined as poem-fragments that tend towards unity by hinting at a centre. It forms a gestalt in the mind of the creative reader. In *Echo's Bones* the centre is supplied by the narrator who is also the central figure in most of the poems. This nameless narrated 'I' can be Beckett himself or an alter-ego like the Belacqua Shuah who dominated Beckett's early fictional landscape. It is not necessary to name the subject because he is Protean. The important point to remember is that this Cartesian self who perceives, is perceived and narrates his various selves (changing self) gives these chaotic fragments their stability. The use in these poems, as in the jettisoned ones, of bits of various languages, echoes and other paraphernalia of the obfuscating kind suggests we are in a sense in the presence of a literary construct as fluid as a collage. This is not surprising. Beckett was familiar with the works of modern painters, musicians, the films of Eisenstein etc. He was aware of ideas like montage, pastiche, assemblage, frottage and bricolage. He pushes his art beyond modernism but does not reach the insouciance so essential to postmodernism. *Echo's Bones* exists in a limbo and is a bridge between the former and the latter. One cannot label the sequence neatly, a situation that would have delighted Beckett. But one can say, along with Perloff, that the collection is closer to Pound's constructivism and Surrealism's fluidity than to Eliot's later style or Wallace Stevens's chiselled post-symbolist high modernism.

The poems in the order of their appearance are "The Vulture," "Enueg I" and "Enueg II," "Alba," "Dortmunder," "Sanies I" and II, "Serena I," II and III "Malacoda," "Da Tagte Es" and "Echo's Bones." Before discussing them the significance of the title — taken from Ovid's version of the legend of Echo in his Metamorphosis — needs to be explained. The choice of title hints at the many-sidedness of Beckett's thematic concerns in the poems and also his impression that he or Art is unable to do justice to them. Echo saw Narcissus and fell in love with him. But Narcissus did not notice her as he was busy gazing at his reflection in the pool. Echo pined away. All that was left of her was her voice. Her bones turned to stone. The story is about unrequited love, failure, sorrow, narcissism and metamorphoses. The poems are, similarly, the residuum of equally vital tales and urges. They are the ciphers of a poet's experiences but they are only traces of their irrecoverable antecedent reality.

The first poem in the collection, "The Vulture," is excellent. It is based on Goethe's lyric "Hazreise im Winter" (Winter in the Harz Mountains). In Goethe's poem the vulture is a simile for his poetic prowess that has the ability to soar. Beckett's vulture is different from the idealized one in Goethe's song.

THE VULTURE

dragging its hunger through the sky
of my skull shell of sky and earth

stooping to the prone who must
soon take up their life and walk

mocked by a tissue that may not serve
till hunger earth and sky be offal.[2]

The poem is characterized by lucid indeterminacy. Any attempt at interpretation becomes subjective and reductive, at the expense of alternate readings that could be equally valid. This is Beckett's and 'The Vulture's' achievement. The vulture is a translucent, irreducible post-symbolist symbol. It has been variously interpreted to mean the artist, the power of the imagination, death and torment by Harvey, Pilling, Esslin and Fletcher respectively. The reference in the fourth line that may be to one of Christ's miracles *(Matthew* 9.6) or the condition He set those who wanted to become His disciples *(Luke* 9.23) complicates the issue. The word "hunger" in the first line dextrously coupled with the verb "dragging " not only describes the vulture's state but with its metaphoric implications concretizes the literal, mixing it with the figurative in an unusual inversion. The absence of punctuation adds to the ambiguity of the poem since one cannot be certain whether the third couplet follows on from the first or the second. To make a choice in such a situation affects the analysis.

If the vulture is understood as a metaphor for the artistic side of the self, its hunger is the urge of that part to create. The prone figures in the poem can then be considered as the objects or people that inspire the artistic nature. It must possess, that is, capture, kill and feed upon them if creation is to occur. The objects, in their turn, may resist this 'dying' that will lead to their transformation. They can be subdued only if the desire to create is sublimated and the other objects in the self — "hunger earth and sky," i.e., everything else — become matter for art. The outcome is deferred in the poem. Beckett's view of the self, the artist, his muse and the raw materials of art are stripped of idealism. His choice of metaphors like "the skull," the vulture," "hunger," "offal" etc., makes this evident. Art seems a *danse macabre* that resembles a surrealistic painting. Suffering is essential for it to thrive. It is based on a fretful dialectic — since the poem is about the process of creation — between a frustrated master and unwilling slaves. This sounds like a religious equation and may be a reason for the Biblical allusions in the poem. The artist, unlike Jesus Christ, is unable to create at will or do miracles. His is a painful attempt at creation rather than a successful one. It involves 'killing,' not dying.

"The Vulture" is a poem that offers much insight into the self in miniature. Influenced by DesCartes' definition of the self — "I think, therefore I am —[3] and Berkeley's "to be is to be perceived,"[4] Beckett incorporates these metaphysical notations into an aesthetic metaphor for the self in his work. In the poem the self perceives, is perceived and narrates its perception of itself without compromising on the complexity of the divisive unity of such a self-reflexive vision. That the self is a composite of many functional selves like the man, the artist etc., and contains in it a vast sensual and sensory universe are also facts revealed in the poem. This intriguing framework of the self in all its variegatedness continues to be explored by Beckett in his later works.

The vulture, the skull and the inner world are motifs that recur in Beckett's works. In 1981 a brief glimpse of "The Vulture" reappears tantalizingly in the last paragraph of Ill Seen Ill Said to confirm that the poem is indeed about artistry, suffering and creating. The text reads:

> "Grant enough remain to devour all, moment by
> glutton moment. Sky earth the whole kit and boodle.
> Not another crumb of carrion left."[5]

The presage of death that was hinted at in the poem is near in this late passage but still deferred. As for the skull and its content, Beckett's awareness that his is an introspective art is constantly stated by him both in his critical works like *Proust* (1931) and in a refrain that runs repeatedly through his works stating with his character Molloy: "It is in the head."[6] In "Cascando," the radio-play of 1962, the sentences by Opener qualify and contradict this awareness of inwardness, replacing it by another that suggests the artist is a selective medium. Opener: "They . . . say it's in his head . . . I don't answer any more. I open and close."[7] In *How It Is* (1964) the narrator makes this idea more explicit with his "I say it as I hear it".[8] But it must be kept in mind that, as in Henry James's novels, Beckett's narrators may also be 'fallible.'

All this is only a partial reading of the poem. "The Vulture," if not exactly inexhaustible, contains many surprises in it. The word "life" in the fourth line, if considered as a substitute for 'the cross,' may refer indirectly to the Passion. Nuances that, like ripples, spread out in different directions and yet are connected to the centre the poem is manage to destabilize coherent readings of the poem, showing us language's tenacious attempt to signify the transcendental while being incapable in its primeval state of resolving the weaknesses inherent in its own fragile structure. Beckett aids the tendency of language to sink into the morass of unintelligibility as far as it can without ever fully sacrificing its capacity to mean. "The Vulture" is the first example of his relative success in such an anti- or post-structural attempt.

As in "Calvary by Night," the central theme here also is indirectly the Creation and, secondarily, the Crucifixion. The first and the eighth chapters of *Genesis* are definitely the unrecognized source of both these poems. G.M. Hopkins's "The Windhover," based indirectly on the same source, is an example of how similar themes may be treated by different poets to create startling contrasts. Yet if the question of temperament is set apart and that of style is raised Beckett's poem is no doubt as powerful as Hopkins's masterpiece and other poems on birds by people like Ted Hughes who wrote 'Hawk Roosting.'

In "Enueg I," the second poem, the Beckettian motif of the skull reappears in lines twelve and fifty-eight. Thus, in a way, the poem is a continuation taking matters up from where "The Vulture" leaves off. But "Enueg I" is about the inner world of the protagonist only at a remove. It is more about the malevolent appearance the external universe wears to the 'I' of the poem. He perhaps projects such a face on to it due to his pain at being subjected to the experience of nursing helplessly a loved one who is dying. She is Peggy Sinclair, one of Beckett's early loves. The enueg was a Provençal verse-form made up of a list of things that irritated the poet. Enueg means vexation. In keeping with this background Beckett's first enueg, a narrative that is a walk, a journey and a metaphorical voyage, lists the changing natural scenery, each panorama of which vexes the traveller, reflecting the wrath, gloom and despair in his mind. The journey in the poem is through the same Irish landscape employed by Joyce in his short stories and novels. But the difference in atmosphere is marked. Beckett's portrayal reveals his misanthropic bent of mind. Nature appears to be suffering as the result of a 'pathetic fallacy' on his part and the poem is fraught with memorable, but ungainly images of this state of being. This view is a revolt against that of romanticism that usually idealized nature.

The poem starts with the Latin word exeo. Exeo means leave. It marks the beginning of the protagonist's journey. The reason for the quick pained exit of the narrator is explained in the subsequent lines. His "darling" is tubercular, coughing blood and dying in a hospital that has a partially Italian / Dantescan name. We get an idea of where Beckett thinks 'Inferno' exists on earth. He suggests that it is found in hospitals. He also hints that the world itself is one in disguise. Leaving the "home" the protagonist walks over a bridge, past a hoarding into the west. He is moving at the same time into the deeper areas of his mind. The stanza makes this clear.

> Exeo in a spasm
> tired of my darling's red sputum
> from the Portobello Private Nursing Home
> its secret things
> and toil to the crest of the surge of the steep perilous bridge
> and lapse down blankly under the scream of the hoarding
> round the bright stiff banner of the hoarding
> into a black west
> throttled with clouds.[9] (1. 1-9)

Throughout the rest of the poem the sights the narrator sees are brilliantly described by making full use of learned, unusual metaphors. The themes he meditates on show misanthropy in full flood. But the sensitive eye for detail and the turn of phrase that is both original and serves its intent redeems this bent.

The second stanza is an 'objective correlative' for rage at a destiny that seems implacable and indifferent to the suffering individual's plight. The image "my skull" interrupts the text effectively here, giving the reader the idea that the poems in the collection are connected but also to intensify the awareness that the poet's anguish is metaphysical in origin. It is related to the question of why misery exists in the world.

> Above the mansions the algum-trees
> the mountains
> my skull sullenly
> clot of anger
> skewered aloft strangled in the cang of the wind
> bites like a dog against its chastisement.[10] (1. 10-15)

While an ascent takes place in the poem, in the poet's mind anger does not permit him a corresponding inner buoyancy. This is revealed in a complicated metaphor that includes calling the skull a blood-clot and the body a skewer. A cang is a "heavy wooden-board worn around the neck as punishment in China."[11] Its etymology is the Vietnamese 'canga' that means yoke. The wind and the body, compared to instruments of torture and imprisonment, imply destiny. This is the first appearance of the image "the wind." It weaves in and out of the poem as an important but unpleasant motif. Its effect on the narrator is consistently irritating. Stanza three finds the walker parallel to the Liffey, a canal in Ireland. The state of the nation and Christianity there seems to be hinted at.

> I trundle along now rapidly on my ruined feet
> flush with the livid canal;

> at Parnell Bridge a dying barge
> carrying a cargo of nails and timber
> rocks itself softly in the foaming cloister of the lock;
> on the far bank a gang of down and outs would seem
> to be mending a beam.[12] (1.16-21)

The alliteration in the first line of the above stanza is worth noting as an example of the meaning of what is said actually entering the rhythm of the line because of the sound of the words. Here form and content become, for an instant, inseparable. The line brings to mind Beckett's Belacqua. The latter is described in "Dante and the Lobster" as one "who had a spavined gait, his feet were in ruins, he suffered with them almost continuously."[13] In *Waiting for Godot* Estragon's feet are in a similar state.

One cannot affirm that the mention of Parnell is apolitical. But from Beckett's writings no leaning in favour of home-rule can be routed out, as it can be from Yeats's or Joyce's. The "nails and timber" refer to the cross. In *Molloy* these lines are echoed. There are so many references to Christ and the Crucifixion in Beckett because he seems to consider life a similarly slow painful death. He is "Christ-haunted."[14] The lines in *Molloy* read:

> I got down, I put my foot to the ground better to see the approaching barge, so gently approaching that the water was unruffled. It was a cargo of nails and timber on its way to some carpenter I suppose.[15]

The last line of the third stanza brings to mind lines from T.S. Eliot's first chorus in "Choruses from The Rock" (1934): "Where the beams are rotten / We will build with new timbers."[16] In "The Rock" these lines are spoken by workmen. Eliot contrasts unemployment with working for God. Beckett catches a glimpse of Eliot's vision but passes by. The mood of the poem darkens. The images become uglier.

Then for miles only wind
and the weals creeping alongside
and the world opening up to the south
across a travesty of champaign to the mountains
and the stillborn evening turning a filthy green
manuring the night fungus
and the mind annulled
wrecked in wind.[17] (1. 22-29)

The above portion is self-explanatory but three points can be made regarding it. The first is the appearance of the leitmotif of "wind" twice. The second point is that the reference to the mind is to the internal universe in the skull, as in "The Vulture." It parallels the external world and it seems clear that both affect each other equally. The images in the stanza, like many in the rest of the poem, are remarkable for their virulent rejection of beauty. There is barely suppressed violence in them and hatred towards life and Nature. The choice of a metaphor like "weals" for ripples of water, adjectives like "travesty," "stillborn" and "filthy," and verbs like "creeping," "manuring," "annulled" and "wrecked" serves to intensify this impression.

The fourth stanza introduces the figure of Democritus. Beckett's description of him is interesting.

I splashed past a little wearish old man,
Democritus,
scuttling along between a crutch and a stick,
His stump caught up horribly, like a claw,
under his breech, smoking.[18] (1. 30-34)

Democritus was called the laughing philosopher. His famous statement, 'nought is more real than nothing,' has influenced Beckett. It is misquoted in his *Murphy*.[19] The appearance of his name in "Enueg I" is no doubt significant. But it is difficult to gauge the exact nature of that significance. Democritus was a metaphysician more radical than Socrates because he was of the opinion that even Socrates's discovery that he knew something because he at least knew that he knew nothing was invalid. Democritus held that even such knowledge is impossible! Beckett holds the same view.

Beckett's character Molloy seems a refinement on his "Democritus." In fact many of Beckett's famous tramp-like creations resemble this old man, being physically handicapped and social outcasts. He may be considered embryonic, a mini-archetype in Beckett's peculiar world.

The introduction of "Democritus" in the poem coincides with that of another important theme in the collection, that of the voyage. The suggestion that the walk / the journey has become a voyage, metaphorically, comes to the reader through the verb "splashed" in line thirty. The description of Democritus also implies this. He resembles a crustacean. He scuttles and has a stump like a claw. His crutch and stick could serve, if occasion arose, as pincers or oars. He is crab-like. The voyage is devoid of epic proportions and the dignity the ancient voyager could bring to it with his heroism. It is also bereft of the excitement of the quest since it has no hope of resolution.

The theme of exile is brought into the foreground in the next section of the poem. The Cartesian antinomies of the self and the world are placed in contrast. The world implies a network of personal relationships to which the individual is attracted but he is unable to be a part of this complex web because his sensitivity makes of him an outsider. The note struck is existentialist in origin. The section deals with three distinct situations. On the narrator's left a game, presumably of football, attracts his attention as a spectacle that is both audible and colourful.

> Then because a field on the left went up in a sudden blaze
> of shouting and urgent whistling and scarlet blue ganzies
> I stopped and climbed the bank to see the game.[20] (1. 35-37)

The picaresque narrative is one in which invariably such seemingly attractive incidents eventually turn out to be "sloughs of despond.' The narrator's attraction is to 'sound and fury that may signify nothing.' But the strength of the temptation is such that for a little while his mind is emptied of his private concerns and suffering. The verbs "stopped," "climbed" and "see" denote relief. A child breaks this brief 'aporia.' The conversation that follows is revealing both of the need of man to belong to society and the realization that little children and the solitary cannot enter the kingdom of the world except at the risk of being exiled.

> A child fidgeting at the gate called up:
> "Would we be let in Mister?"
> "Certainly" I said "You would."
> But afraid, he set off down the road.
> "Well" I called after him "Why wouldn't you go on in?"
> "Oh" he said knowingly,
> "I was in that field before and I got put out."[21] (1 38-44)

The hidden Biblical allusion — that of Jesus Christ saying "Except ye be converted and become as a little child ye will not enter the Kingdom of Heaven."[22] — offers no hope for the child or the narrator here in an interesting twist.

The last lines of the section compare the colourful game to two images. The first image refers to Beckett's childhood in Ireland and Moses's meeting with God in the wilderness *(Exodus* 3. 1-6). The second image is both botanical and sexual. The images suggest the range of Beckett's rejection. He recedes from the world, brought to the realization that he is an exile in his own land owing to the differences between his fellow-creatures and himself.

So on,
derelict,
as from a bush of gorse in the mountain after dark,
or in Sumatra the jungle hymen,
the still flagrant rafflesia.[23] (1. 45-49)

The rafflesia is a bright flower found in the jungles of Sumatra. It seems to Beckett to resemble the hymen. The theme of exile is carried into the next stanza to stress its importance. Exile is also an experience that is communal. The community rejects the stranger in their midst but is in turn rejected by the inexplicable at the metaphysical level.

Next:

a lamentable family of grey, verminous hens,
perishing out in the sunken field;
trembling, half-asleep, against the closed door of a shed,
with no means of roosting.[24] (1. 46-50)

The neat reversal whereby the exile has a glimpse of those he is separated from as also being exiled from security in the plural, put in the language of metaphor, is well done. The poem returns to Nature as a malevolent presence. The motifs of the skull, the wind and the voyage return insistently to sensitize the reader to the organic unity of this remarkable fragmented poem.

The great mushy toadstool,
green-black,
oozing up after me,
soaking up the tattered sky like an ink of pestilence,
in my skull the wind going fetid,
the water . . .[25] (1. 51-56)

The latter half of the fourth stanza and this section are linked by the repetition of the description of nature as vile and the incarnation of the narrator's internal state.

The theme of exile is incorporated into the lines of the next stanza again. The world is seen as wearing a mask behind which lies the same suffering the self is going through. Just as the stanza quoted above links up with the fourth stanza to strengthen a vision of Nature that is daemonic rather than idyllic, the stanza that follows unites with the ones already quoted that are on exile to form a clearer picture of the variations on the theme like loneliness, solitude, rejection and suffering.

Next:

> On the hill down from the Fox and Geese into Chapelizod
> a small malevolent goat, exiled on the road,
> remotely pucking the gate of his field;
> the Isolde stores a great perturbation of sweaty heroes,
> in their Sunday best,
> come hastening down for a pint of nepenthe, moly or half and half
> from watching the hurlers above in Kilmainham.[26] (1. 57-64)

The narrator, it is clear, identifies himself with the goat. It is one more metaphor for the feeling of estrangement and the inability or impossibility of escaping from such a strait-jacket. The artificial gaiety of the crowd, who after watching athletics or participating in it have come to a pub, is only a disguise according to the poet since they have private sorrows which they try to drown in alcohol and by leading an active, sociable life. The clue to this point of view is there in the substitution of "nepenthe" and "moly" for whisky and beer in the poem. The latter pair is what is common in Ireland. The former are archaic soporifics. Nepenthe is a drug causing forgetfulness of grief and moly a herb supposedly endowed with magic properties.

The penultimate stanza introduces the note of suicide into the poem only to dismiss it. Death that loomed as a possible threat to the self in stanza one on the "perilous bridge" (1.5) now appears as an invitation that offers no sensible solution to an artist.

Blotches of doomed yellow in the pit of the Liffey;
the fingers of the ladders hooked over the parapet,
soliciting;
a slush of vigilant gulls in the grey spew of the sewer.[27] (1. 65-68)

Beckett's opinion of suicide is given away by the verbs "hooked" and "soliciting." It suggests that suicide involves prostituting life's dignity. The metaphysical conceit of the curved top of the ladder as "fingers" is fine. The introduction of the adjective "vigilant" in the fourth line to describe the attitude of the gulls, who as a result resemble birds of prey like the vulture in the first poem, is also effective.

The poem begins with a reference to Dante's *Inferno* through the echo "its secret things"[28] (1.4), situating it in a literary context. It ends with a similar act of aesthetic distancing by another allusion, this time to lines in Rimbaud's "Barbare" and a note in prose that Rimbaud attached to it[29] in the margin of his text.

Ah the banner
the banner of meat bleeding
on the silk of the seas and the arctic flowers
that do not exist[30] (1. 69-72)

The setting sun and evening sky are scarlet, reminding the reader of the "red sputum" in the second line of the poem. The linear journey is also a circular spiral. It ends near the Liffey in the west. A fierce denial of all hopes — normal and otherwise — is implied by the lines that state that even the archipelagoes of the imagination that an aesthetic seer like Rimbaud had recourse to is finally illusory. All that one can be certain of is the suffering signified by the image of the dying day, sun and sky. The inevitability of the death that will happen to the narrator's beloved is signified. Death is inexorable. The voyage ends on this negative note.

The opening image of the poem simulates birth. It serves the art of the poem well to begin it with. The last image of the evening, one of closure, is also similarly effective. The image of birth keeps returning in Beckett's works, as a beginning. This is especially so in "The Expelled" (pub. 1954). In style and diction the enueg's prosaic, fictional mode is impressive. It is clear that Beckett sought for the apt word and often found it in the uncommon. The use of words like enueg, exeo, cang, champaign, ganzies, pucking, nepenthe, moly etc., reveals his Joycean love for the unusual verbal signifier. The transference of words into new syntactical positions (e.g., "lapse" in six substituted for 'walk'), neologisms (e.g., "manuring") etc., make the lines lively and colloquial as in Browning's and Joyce's works. Puns like "livid canal" that by its sound suggests the name Liffey occur every now and then. All these are common to many of Beckett's early poems and show how in his use of language he attempted to parallel Joyce's method in the different medium of verse.[31]

The third poem in the collection, another enueg, develops the sequence by expanding on the process of dying. The death of love and of the beloved is shown as inevitable in "Enueg I." In "Enueg II" it is seen that one day the lover will also die. Living itself, Beckett implies, is only a euphemism for dying. Suffering, loss, exile and metamorphosis are the inescapable stations on this 'way of the cross' called life. These strands of thought form the core of the poem.

The first three stanzas deal with the image of a cloud against the evening sky that reminds the poet first of his beloved and then of St. Veronica wiping Jesus's face with a cloth on his way to Calvary. In the last stanza of the poem the cloud melts away to reinforce with a natural parallel the passing away of the poet's beloved. In between the first three and last stanzas appear two stanzas that remark on the resemblance living bears to 'the dolorous way.' The poem contains several autobiographical references, the ignorance of which can lead to misreading. As Kenner rightly remarks, much of the poem would seem unwanted if one is not aware of its background. As in "Enueg I," it is Peggy Sinclair's life and death that is being eulogised. "Eneug II" is an elegy for her. This is clearly recognizable. But the other personal reference is not so obvious.

"Eneug II" was written after Beckett resigned his job at Trinity College, Dublin, in 1931 to confluence an aimless period of wandering, disappointing those close to him who expected him to become a brilliant academician. His *Proust* had proved he was capable in such a capacity. He felt that he appeared to them like a prodigal and the act of his leaving was a betrayal a little like that of Judas's. Thus, besides being elegiac, the poem is also a complaint, tentative, unsure, self-incriminatory, against social norms, expectations and responsibilities.

ENUEG II

world world world world
and the face grave
cloud against the evening
de morituri nihil nisi

and the face crumbling shyly
too late to darken the sky
blushing away into the evening
shuddering away like a gaffe
veronica mundi
veronica munda
give us a wipe for the love of Jesus

sweating like Judas
tired of dying
tired of policemen

feet in marmalade
perspiring profusely
heart in marmalade
smoke more fruit
the old heart the old heart
breaking outside congress
doch I assure thee
lying on O'Connell Bridge
goggling at the tulips of the evening
the green tulips
shining round the corner like an anthrax
shining on Guiness's barges

the overtone the face
too late to brighten the sky
doch doch I assure thee[32]

The first line with its repetition of the word "world" reminds us that "the world is too much with us."[33] The deathly and deadly aspects of life are brought in by the punon the word "grave" in the second line. The unfinished Latintag is from Catullus and means "of the dying nothing except."[34] That the face is a woman's becomes clear through the verbs in stanza three. The cloud crumbles "shyly" and "blushes."

The face-like cloud spread out on the banner of the sky reminds the narrator of the imprint Jesus's face left on St. Veronica's towel; an image wrought by his sweat and the blood dripping from his forehead crowned with thorns. "Munda" means 'neat' and "mundi," 'of the world,' according to Kenner.[35] The narrator longs for solace since he feels that he is in the same situation as the Lord. The experience of dying is painful to both God and man.

Having hinted that his life too is a 'via dolorosa' a little like that of Jesus's, the fifth stanza finds the central character elaborating on his journey to death. Realism and a wry sense of humour is present in these lines. The onomatopoeic rhythm of walking enters them. In his self the narrator finds a similarity not only to Jesus in that they both suffer but also to Judas in that they both know fear. Belacqua Shuah has a more vivid realization of the latter resemblance in *Dream*. It is also hinted at in "Casket of Pralinen. . . ." The present narrator's sins include rebellion, smoking, overeating and an irrational hatred of life and Nature. He lies down, reminiscent of Jesus's fall because of the weight of the heavy wooden cross. The sight of green tulips invades his consciousness looking like anthrax, a disease sheep catch. Green, as in "Enueg I," is antithetical to hope. The reference to anthrax is significant in that it reminds us that Beckett often considered himself as a lamb being unwillingly led through life to death; a kind of sacrificial slaughter. The religious allusion is covert. Hinted at in "Home Olga," it is made more clearly in the later "Ooftish" (1938). The barge in "Enueg I" has become barges. They do not carry the pre-requisites from which the cross is made. Instead, they are filled with Irish beer. This, while not a permanent antidote to suffering, is perhaps a temporary and temporal respite. In the course of the stanza not only does the narrator's feet turn to jelly but his heart also follows suit. "Congress" suggests union, the impossibility of which, whether with God, the lover or the dead, creates sorrow.

In the last stanza, instead of a compassionate face like Veronica's, he sees the cloud vanish above him. The face-like cloud that might have given him shade by darkening the sky while he walked or the strength to carry on by brightening the sky refuses to oblige him. The narrator suggests that like the cloud the beloved's life seems to have been a discontinuous fragment. It is like the incompleteness of the Latin quotation in the poem. Her meaning, the author suggests with ill-repressed irony, is that she was a "gaffe." An assurance of this fact that she was a mistake is given to the reader by his use of the German word for the strong positive, 'doch,' the nearest equivalent of which is the weaker English 'yes.' What is left to the lover is not the consolation a Veronica stands for but memories. The poem resembles the enueg only in its fourth stanza. Harvey writes:

> . . . .Beckett's enuegs are really closer to another Provençal form, the planh, which is a poem expressing the great displeasure and sorrow one feels at loss or misfortune. . .[36]

But the use of discontinuous form and the list in the fourth stanza makes this modern revival similar to the enueg. The policemen in the poem appear in the singular in the short story "A Wet Night " as a symbol of the sort of authoritarian tyranny Beckett resented and tried to escape from when he gave up 'the groves of academe' and opted to become a creative writer.

"Alba," the title of the fourth poem, means aubade or dawn-song. It also means white or 'the white one' in the Latin and is the name of a woman character in Beckett's *Dream* and *MPTK*. The albada is related to the serenade and the nocturne. It was written, set to music and sung by Provençal troubadours either to complain of the coming of dawn, an unwelcome intrusion to lovers, or to celebrate the dawn as a symbol of hope and the resurrection. Beckett's alba is based on the aesthetic type. It is in reaction to the religious alba. His alba is a recapitulation of a night of love that occurs in the imagination of the narrator, written in the absence of the occasion that is looked forward to but also, imaginatively speaking, over. This convoluted note of expectation and fulfilment is conveyed by the present tense the poem is written in. The counterpoints to the main theme, eroticism, are found in the first stanza and the latter end of the last. The encroaching dawn acts as a backdrop to make the lovers aware of the transience of the act. The title has another reference embedded in it. In the short story "A Wet Night" one of Belacqua Shuah's amorous flings is with a lady named the Alba Perdue (the lost, white one). The story introduces her and Belacqua's adventures with her resemble those in the poem.

ALBA

before morning you shall be here
and Dante and the Logos and all strata and mysteries
and the branded moon
beyond the white plane of music
that you shall establish here before morning
grave suave singing silk
stoop to the black firmament of areca
rain on the bamboos flower of smoke alley of willows
who though you stoop with fingers of compassion
to endorse the dust
shall not add to your bounty
whose beauty shall be a sheet before me
a statement of itself drawn across the tempest of emblems
so that there is no sun and no unveiling and no host
only I and then the sheet
and bulk dead[37]

"Alba," as it was initially written by Beckett in 1931, is different from this version but the variations are slight. The commas and the punctuation marks have been dropped. "For" in line nine is changed to "with," "sign" in line ten to "endorse" and "cannot" in line eleven to "shall not." These changes, especially the second one, improve the poem. There is a corresponding gain in clarity. The poem records a refusal on the part of the narrator to carry the theme of eroticism into the realm of transcendence by giving it too much importance. If he will not be an ethical poet, neither will he be the bard of Eros.

The beginning and end of the first stanza strikes the bell of arriving morn to point us to the title and the form being employed. The stanza itself cannot be understood without reference to Beckett's *Dream* and his short story "Dante and the Lobster." Belacqua, in the beginning of that story, cannot discern the nature of spiritual truth and in frustration he chooses the sensual world. This is hedonism. Similarly, questions of salvation, discipleship, mercy, justice and pity — "Dante and the Logos and all strata and mysteries / and the branded moon" — disturb the present narrator and he opts instead for a "white plane of music" he wants the Alba to establish for him.

The second stanza describes, by way of a musical metaphor that is Chinese in origin, the beauty of the act of sex which is amoral like the art of music. Areca is the wood from which a Chinese musical instrument is made.

The third stanza is ambiguous. The woman seems to have turned into a benevolent threat, a feminine Christ-like figure reminiscent of the compassionate Christ who forgave the adulteress and dispersed the crowd baying for her blood *(The Gospel of John* 8:1-11). Beckett turns away from this Beatrice-like apparition. He prefers amorous experience to the person who offers him the same and embraces the self and death as a replacement for love and the adjustments required in marriage. It would not be far-fetched to say that the woman in the poem strikes the artist as a metaphor for a way to the truth and in it Beckett stands revealed as an artist who, though he has no faith in art, steadfastly refuses to be either a religious saint or a secular one. His desire is for experience and then for an aftermath where deeds are subsumed away and only the stasis of death remains. The self is glorified and so are Art and Death. Beckett seems to consider the nature of death-in-life the absolute in terms of quasi-mystical experience and any event such as coitus that stimulates this attracts his attention. It may be interesting to point out that the word "stoop" which appeared first in "The Vulture" reappears with the same intensity twice in "Alba." The poem introduces three motifs that become prevalent in the collection. They are "beauty," "the sheet" and the word "dead." "Silk" and "grave" are repetitions that signify the same meanings they had in the first contexts they appeared, in the enuegs. The colours "white" and "black" work like a musical thesis and antithesis within the poem. There is no synthesis. The word "suave" reappears in a later poem, "Sanies I," in as illuminating a context. This network of links slowly strengthens the collection into an autonomous entity, as do the allusions that are constantly Provençal, Dantescan, Biblical and Beckettian.

The next poem in the collection, "Dortmunder," is closely related to "Alba" in theme and texture. It expands and alters the position of the former, making its meaning more specific.

DORTMUNDER

In the magic the Homer dusk
past the red spire of sanctuary
I null she royal hulk
hasten to the violet lamp to the thin K'in music of the bawd.
She stands before me in the bright stall
sustaining the jade splinters
the scarred signaculum of purity quiet
the eyes the eyes black till the plagal east
shall resolve the long night phrase.
Then, as a scroll, folded,
and the glory of her dissolution enlarged
in me, Habakkuk, mard of all sinners.
Schopenhauer is dead, the bawd
puts her lute away.[38]

"Dortmunder" was written by Beckett in Kassel, in Germany when he was drunk. It is clearly another dawn-song. Dortmunder is the name of a German beer. The atmosphere of the serenade, the nocturne and the alba soak the poem. 'Wander jahre,'

Beckett's experience of the years since 1931, is hinted at by the shift in scene from Dublin to Germany. The spires in Germany are often red in colour. The second stanza seems to be set in an exotic motel. John Pilling speculates that the "I" in it is Belacqua but there is no internal evidence to prove such a conjecture. It is a theory that could be more relevant where "Alba" is concerned. But the woman is still the Alba.

At several points the poem is similar to "Alba." The rejection of religion, the presence of Chinese music, the night of love and the certainty that dawn will bring the proceedings to a close are all repetitions. There is an ambience, created by the words in the poem, of profane mysticism. From the pagan beginning which causes the narrator of the poem to praise Homer and walk past a church in a rejection of Eliot's "Only / There is shadow under this red rock. / (Come in under the shadow of this red rock.),"[39] accompanied by a woman who is willing to have sex with him, the poem narrates a sexual experience that attempts to reach out to a significance beyond itself. The reference to Schopenhauer is the vital clue. In *Proust*, Beckett states the German philosopher's definition of the artistic procedure: "The contemplation of the world independently of the principle of reason."[40] He paraphrases Schopenhauer on music: is the Idea itself, unaware of the world of phenomena, existing ideally outside the universe, apprehended not in Space and Time only, and consequently untouched by the teleological hypothesis."[41] The poem is an effort to capture an experience that parallels such music in a medium, language, that opposes this tendency in art. The logos is opposed to the aesthetic ethos. The resultant failure is symbolized at the end of the poem where the bawd (bard) relinquishes the lute.

That the literature of aesthetic mysticism based on amoral intensity leads to art of the calibre of the poems of Baudelaire cannot be denied. But its success is limited because it cannot negate the conflict between life and Art. This tension creates the ambivalent note in both "Alba" and "Dortmunder." Beckett resolves it by opting for Art while being forced to concede his failure to meet the demands of life. The woman in "Dortmunder" is merely an excuse for the artistic experiment, a devolution from his image of the woman in the enueg-poems. This is not progress but stasis and degeneration, except in the struggle for new form to evoke what cannot be expressed. Bacchanalianism and Art are deified at the expense of truth and life in these two poems that haunt the reader with their aesthetic ability. The reference to Habakkuk does not fit into the poem as neatly as that of Schopenhauer.

The angst prevalent in "The Vulture" and the enuegs is subdued in "Alba" and Dortmunder." But it reappears in "Sanies I." Sanies is "a watery, vital body fluid esp., one comparable to blood."[42] The imaginative title is also the herald of a new form of poetry. The sanies are poems that simulate the qualities of gaseousness and liquidness. "Sanies I" has a freewheeling structure in which Beckett's birth, his parents, Dublin, Foxrock (the place where Beckett was born in 1906), a bicycle-ride, memories of his immediate and ancient past mixed with fantasy and the decisive rejection of the woman of the "Alba" and "Dortmunder" poems form the focal points. The language of the poem is onomatopoeic and mimics both the motion of the bicycle and the resultant jerky thought-pattern of the rider. The rhythm, though unattractive, is audible. To quote examples:

> pounding along in three ratios like a sonata (1.3)
>
> Potwalloping now through the promenaders
> this trusty all-steel this super-real (1. 10-11)
>
> belting along in the meantime clutching the bike[43] (1.16)

The poem deals with Beckett's temporary return to Ireland. This explains the reference to the prodigal son in two of its lines:

> bound for home like a good boy[44] (1.12)
>
> good as gold now in the prime after a brief prodigality[45] (1. 35)

In "Enueg II" the hint that the narrator is a prodigal had already appeared. In "Alba" and "Dortmunder" his experiences as a prodigal are written about. In "Sanies I" the result of his sojourn is given:

> tired now hair ebbing gums ebbing ebbing home
> . . . .
> yea and suave
> suave urbane beyond good and evil
> biding my time without rancour you may take your oath
> distraught half-crooked . . .[46] (1. 33, 34-38a)

Despite the fact that his stay in alien lands seems to have made him less civilized the narrator shows no sign of wanting to prolong his return since he rejects the values of the place that he was born in. The 'suaveness' of the woman in "Alba" has entered his soul and it no longer thirsts for innocent pleasures.

This 'sanie' and the poems that follow are full of details that those who have read *MPTK* are familiar with. Cycling, for instance, is a motif that appears in many of Beckett's works. Belacqua Shuah, Molloy, Moran, Malone and even Mercier and Camier had bicycles. Similarly, Beckett's Freudian love of the womb-tomb spoken of in "Sanies I" is also Belacqua's. In "Fingal," Belacqua says: "I want very much to be back in the caul, on my back in the dark forever."[47] In "Sanies I," this appears as: "ah to be back in the caul now with no trust / no fingers no spoilt love."[48] (1. 14-15)

There is an amusing snap-shot of the self in the poem:" pot-valiant caulless waisted in rags hatless"[49] (1. 18). Beckett describes his birth in a manner reminiscent of Lawrence Sterne's and Jonathan Swift's, indulging in black humour.

> oh the larches the pain drawn like a cork
> the glans he took the day off up hill and down dale
> with a ponderous fawn from the Liverpool London and Globe
> back the shadows lengthen the sycamores are sobbing
> to roly-poly oh to me a spanking boy
> buckets of fizz childbed is thirsty work
> for the midwife he is gory
> for the proud parent he washes down a gob of gladness
> for footsore Achates also he pants his pleasure
> sparkling beestings for me[50] (1. 23-32)

This amusing prosaic narrative of the imagination suggests more than it says. Both the pain and the joy that accompanies birth finds a place in it.

As in "Casket of Pralinen. . .," the technique of self-reflexive versifying is made use of in "Sanies I." In the midst of the journey-voyage that is being narrated aline appears that breaks the illusion of the verse being reality reported as it is. Beckett writes: "I see main verb at last"[51] (1. 34). It is again metaverse stirring in the background.

The poem "Sanies I" ends with the passage where the temptation that woman, sex and love offers is rejected because Beckett seems to dislike marriage, conjugal felicity and the idea of producing offspring. This is an inference based on what goes on before in the poem. As in Alba," the woman appears in the guise of a feminine Christ-like figure, reminiscent of the powerful Christ who could walk on water (The Gospel of John 6. 19). Just as the girl in "Enueg I" and II is the Smeraldina-Rima or Peggy Sinclair, the woman in "Alba," "Dortmunder" and "Sanies I" is the Alba Perdue of *Dream* and *MPTK.* She is not the symbol of innocence but she is not exactly the symbol of the harlot either. She is a woman who unabashedly expresses the archetypal feminine desires for sex, love, marriage and children for which she ruthlessly seeks a suitable mate. To this end she gives of herself and her body freely. To the artist she seems like a deceiver, hiding behind her seeming forwardness a subtly traditional invitation that he wants to escape from. He says in the last section of the poem:

> her whom alone in the accusative
> I have dismounted to love
> gliding towards me dauntless nautch-girl on the face of the waters
> dauntless daughter of desires in the old black and flamingo
> get along with you now take the six the seven the eight or the little single-dekker
> take a bus for all I care cadge a lift
> home to the cob of your web in Holles Street
> and let the tiger go on smiling
> in our hearts that funds ways home[52] (1. 44-52)

The ego of the narrator does not permit him to give in to the desire to lead a normal marital life in Ireland.

"Sanies II" is set in Paris. The prodigal has exiled himself again. A story of bohemian days, it is placed in and around a bar or brothel and includes a flagellation-scene. This bizarre pornographic episode unfolds to its distasteful finale in the midst of linguistic bric-a-brac that borders easily on the fantastic in keeping with the air of unreality that permeates the whole poem. The obscenity is kept in check by the playfulness of the language. The narrator feels fresh after a bath and goes fora walk. He goes to the "American Bar" and indulges in masochism at the hands of a woman. The poet envies Dante who was once like him, but: "lo Alighieri has got off au revoirto all that / I break down quite in a titter of despite"[53] (1. 27-28). The poem ends sombrely with an incomplete 'kyrie eleison.' It is ambiguous. One does not know if it is placed there because of the poet's awareness that while the lifestyle of the decadent aesthete that includes sexual perversion may lead to art of a high order it bodes ill for his psyche. Perhaps it is only ironic. The poem stretches itself close to the point of utter chaos but, surprisingly enough, a thread of clarity remains. This may be the contribution of the sanie as a form, that it has all the fluidity of the body's secretions without losing their cohesiveness. "Sanies II" is perhaps the weakest poem in *Echo's Bones* though it is a bit difficult to decipher.

The two sanies are followed by three serenas. Traditionally, the serenade was an evening song. The idea that it is romantic and meant to be sung or played by a lover is a later encrustation. Beckett both returns to the original tradition and changes it. His serenades are poems set in the evening. In "Serena I" the narrator is in London. A visit to the zoo, a religious aside, a journey by various conveyances, memories of Ireland and a conclusion form its content. The poem splits the narrator into the observer and the observed, making it clear that the Cartesian subject is also an observable object, not only to others but also to himself. Berkeley is responsible, as in "Beckett's "Film" (1963), for Beckett abstracting this insight. Thus one of the facts about the self hinted at in "The Vulture" is clearly outlined here.

> I find me taking the Crystal Palace (1. 21)
>
> I surprise me moved by the many a funnel hinged (1. 27)
>
> then I hug me below among the canaille[54] (1. 35)

The first two quotations clarify that the self can be irrational in its actions at times.

In the first stanza of "Serena I" Beckett re-states his un-Romantic approach to Nature by quoting the Grecian Pantheist Thales and then attaching to his famous saying his footnote in a line of verse that foregrounds the universality of suffering. He writes: "All things full of gods/ pressed down and bleeding"[55] (1. 67). The effect is subversive. In the zoo he watches wary animals and feels homesick seeing their imprisoned plight. Homesickness is an unusual phenomenon for Beckett but it is clearly spelt out in this poem. The climax of the visit to the zoo is that he gets a chance to watch an adder swallow a rat. Belacqua's voyeurism, better explained in the short story "Walking Out" and Apollinaire's influence on Beckett's verse find their echoes in "Serena I." But the main thread seems to be the issue of private suffering that finds a parallel in the experiences the anti-hero goes through. They are of a slight but thoroughly irritating nature. As in many of his weak poems like "Sanies II," Beckett's "Serena I" ends with powerful lines. In "Serena I" the last stanza has special significance because it was written and added on after a gap of six months and shows a difference in maturity.

> my brother the fly
> the common housefly
> sidling out of darkness into light
> fastens on his place in the sun
> whets his legs
> revels in his planes his poisiers
> it is the autumn of his life
> he could not serve typhoid and mammon. (1. 46-53)

The last line is a quotable 'echo' but resists interpretation. Beckett was hardly twenty-nine years when he wrote these lines. They are prophetic of the attitude of his later characters to life's paradoxes. Disease and matter seem to be the two poles life is built around, according to Beckett. He considers both equally distasteful. But the former is unavoidable. Disease seems to win out more often than the latter. Imprisonment in place, in time and in the self are all protested against futilely in "Serena I."

"Serena II" is a poem about the narrator's childhood and his native land. In "Sanies I" a glimpse that Beckett's childhood was a happy one was given. He writes: "Happy days snap the stem shed a tear."[56] In "Serena II" his happy childhood is contrasted with what he has become and the result is poignant. The poem describes a visit by the narrator one evening to the place of his birth. The reaction to his return there is violently intense as hatred for the place and regret for what is lost are balanced in the last lines by a hopeless realism that is probably the bleakest tone available to the literature of our time. Beckett's vision of Ireland is one available only to himself. It is obvious that Foxrock was loved by him deeply in his childhood. In growing up, the lustre is lost. All that is left to him is what cannot be recovered. In superb lines reminiscent of Dylan Thomas's style, without the awkwardness of introducing neologisms, Beckett describes the ideal past in a scene similar to Christ's second temptation by the devil *(Luke* 4. 9-13). Ireland is personified as a woman.

> she took me up onto a watershed
> whence like the rubrics of childhood
> behold Meath shining through a chink in the hills
> posses of larches there is no going back on
> a rout of tracks and streams fleeing to the sea
> kindergartens of steeples and then the harbour
> like a woman making to cover her breasts
> and left me (1. 27-34)

He narrates the present:

> it is worse than dream (1.41)
> the toads abroad again on their rounds

sidling up to their snares
the fairy tales of Meath ended.[57] (1. 50-52)

The poem rejects retrogression into the ideal landscape of the world as pictured through the eyes of a child. Nationality, the religion one is born with, escapism, love of nature etc., are all empty of attraction for Beckett. But he is keenly aware of the value of these traditional norms and what he loses in turning away from them. He suggests his rejection is due to the fact that, like Echo's bones, they have become insubstantial ghosts or stony. Like Dylan Thomas's poems on childhood, especially "Poem in October," "Serena II" is a classic expression of nostalgia. In *Echo's Bones* it is perhaps the best of the longer poems. It makes one aware that modern poetry, though it breaks the norms of prosody and is difficult because of private or hermetic allusions, is capable of being highly expressive and communicative when it finds the balance between freedom and rigour.

Like all the poems from "Enueg I" the next poem in the collection, "Serena III" is intimately connected with *Dream* and *MPTK*. The first couplet explains that Beauty is beyond the reach of even the expressive artist and it is the hope that it may one day be captured that keeps him going. The lines read: "Fix this pothook of beauty on this palette/ you never know it might be final"[58] (1. 1-2). The view that woman, love and sex may be a private route to personal, earthly salvation is again abandoned in this poem: "Or leave her she is paradise and then / plush hymens on your eyeballs"[59] (1. 3-4). The lines are also connected to the ideal of Beauty which like woman, sex and the concept of love is, on closer examination, not a transcendent reality. This undoes one of the strongholds the narrator posited in "Alba," i.e., traditional Art's belief in its power.

Most of the next two stanzas of the poem where the protagonist is seen to be moving through streets with names that suit his thoughts, like "Misery Hill" — Beckett's use of real place names in the poems of *Echo's Bones* to produce such poetic effects is commendable — can be understood only in relation to a passage in "Ding Dong" in *MPTK.* It also throws light on the incessant necessity of the protagonist throughout the poems in *Echo's Bones* to keep journeying.

My sometime friend Belacqua enlivened the last phase of his solipsism, before he toed the line and began to relish the world, with the belief that the best thing he had to do was to move constantly from place to place.[60]

In "Serena III" his movement finally brings him face to face with the compassion of Jesus Christ *(The Gospel of John* 8. 1-11), the most disturbing challenge an artist meets. But the narrator's principle of unrest leads him to say:

> the sands quicken in your hot heart
> hide yourself not in the Rock keep on the move
> keep on the move[61] (1. 25-27)

Eliot's position is different. Beckett's lines remind one of, perhaps an apt memory, Thom Gunn's "On the Move":

> At the worst one is in motion and at best
> Reaching no absolute in which to rest
> One is nearer by not keeping still.[62] (1. 38-40)

Beckett's lines are influenced by A.M. Toplady's famous hymn, "Rock of Ages":

> Rock of Ages, cleft for me
> Let me hide myself in Thee[63] (1. 1,2)

This is an example of how verse can influence even antagonists of the ideological school it belongs to because it is dependent for its effect not just on content but its ability to haunt the reader's mind with the power of its unforgettable syntactic arrangements.

In the preceding poems, except for "The Vulture," the influence of Joyce and modernism is prevalent. But in the last three poems the tone we now recognize as being more Beckettian emerges. The poem "Malacoda," even as it pays a tribute to Dante in its tripartite structure and some of its allusions, is primarily a Beckettian elegy written to commemorate the death of his father in 1933. Malacoda means 'evil-tail' in Italian and is one of the grotesque demons in Dante's *Inferno*. In the poem he or it comes as an errand-runner from the underworld to take the dead body of the father with him. This is figurative. Literally, he is a man from the undertaker and has come to measure the body for the coffin's size. He brings with him, as they take the coffined body on its last journey, another devil; the hearse-driver called Scarmilion. The narrator of the poem, the son, appears detached throughout but the unveiling of the allusions in the poem shows that this apparent distance is only a mask.

MALACODA

thrice he came
the undertaker's man
impassible behind his scutal bowler
to measure
is he not paid to measure
this incorruptible in the vestibule
this malebranca knee-deep in the lilies
Malacoda knee-deep in the lilies
Malacoda for all the expert awe
that felts his perineum mutes his signal
sighing up through the heavy air

must it be it must be it must be
find the weeds engage them in the garden
hear she may see she need not

to coffin
with assistant ungulata
find the weeds engage their attention
hear she must see she need not

to cover
to be sure cover cover all over
your targe allow me hold your sulphur
divine dogday glass set fair
stay Scarmilion stay stay
lay this Huysum on the box
mind the imago it is he
hear she must see she must

all aboard all souls half-mast aye aye nay[64]

Malacoda comes thrice to the house of mourning. On the first occasion he measures, the second time he coffins and in the end he covers. The body is kept in a room filled with lilies presumably gifted by mourners. The son experiences varying emotions that include distaste for Malacoda and his job, grief and the desire to lessen the same for his mother. The desire to understand Death and fittingly honour the memory of his father who is "the imago" is also a part of this complex situation. Failure is the theme that runs through the lines. The father's failure is implied in the fact that Death reduces him to a corpse and leaves him at the mercy of people like the undertaker who make a living off it. The mother, ex-wife and new widow, has to undergo the bitter experience of seeing her husband's body being coffined and carried away from her in permanent separation. The son succeeds neither in sparing his mother the pain nor in paying an adequate tribute to the hallowed memory of the father he honours. All he can do is place a painting of butterflies / flowers on the lid of the box in farewell. He sees the coffin as a ship setting out on a voyage. An 'imago' is a son's idealized picture of the father. Huysum's painting suggests that the narrator feels that his father has undergone chrysalis. In his mind too a whole set of relationships and concepts are facing a similar metamorphosis. The overwhelming nature of Death from which there is no escape dawns on him. The last lines reveal that Beckett does not believe in immortality. They deny the hope of even an eternity in hell. Death can be resisted by Beckett only through Art. The metonym "the weeds " and the repetitions of the "must it be it must be it must be" and the "hear she . . . see she . . . " refrain add to this serious poem's effect.

The implied image of the chariot brings to mind Emily Dickinson's famous poem "Because I could not stop for Death."[65] There Death is written of as a first-hand experience. The penultimate poem in *Echo's Bones*, "Da Tagte Es" (Then the Dawn), while paradoxical as to the narrator's identity, can be read as a poem that, like Dickinson's, reports Death from a similar view whereby through the imagination the narrator explains what it is like for both the dead and the mourner. "Da Tagte Es" is also a communal lament for the living and of the dead and is the best poem in the collection. The title is taken from one of Walther von der Vogelweide's 'tagelieds' (dawn-songs) in the German. It draws on the religious alba for its form. But its content is in reaction to the same. In the religious dawn-song morn is a symbol of hope, signifying the triumph of good over evil and Christ's Resurrection. In Beckett's albas it comes as an unwelcome interruption or, as here, as a sign of permanent loss.

> redeem the surrogate goodbyes
> the sheet a stream in your hand

who have no more for the land
the glass unmisted above your eyes[66]

The poem is so fine that all its nuances cannot be wrung from it. Its connection to "Alba," where also "the sheet" is mentioned as a pun for the winding-cloth the body is wrapped in, is clear. It is linked via the motif of the voyage to all the poems where the voyage is suggested. In its use of the word "glass" and its third line it is connected to "Malacoda." It is connected directly to "Malacoda" even otherwise since it is a communal elegy for all the dead, including Beckett's father.

One cannot ascertain who the speaker is. Is it the departed one or the one left behind on the shore? Life is seen as a constant preparation through many farewells for the final parting in the first line. But Death seems redemptive since there is nothing put on or false about it. Does the sheet refer to Veronica's cloth as in "Enueg I" or the shroud that the poet wished for in "Alba" that the body should be wrapped in? The skewed syntax helps in withholding the poems mysteries and secrets. The glass may refer to the fineness of the weather indirectly since it is "unmisted" and also to the fact that the dead are saved the trouble of weeping. Literally, it is the lid of the coffin. Charon, the boatman across the Styx, is also implicated as in "Malacoda" dimly. Lyrical and impenetrable, "Da TagteEs" is a revelation that language can be used in such a way that it is complete but perennially translucent. This is Beckett's original contribution to language and poetry, exemplified by this poem and "The Vulture."

The last poem, "Echo's Bones," tries to sustain the tempo of its forerunner but fails. It acts as a partially efficient summary of the collection. As it says in its fourth line, "the gantelope" (gauntlet/gamut) "of sense and nonsense" has been "run"[67] in the previous poems. Echo's voice, sanies, bones and visions have all been made available to the reader, transcreated, i.e., metamorphosed into the modern context. The narrator, compulsive walker that he is, is found at the end to be still walking frenetically. "DaTagte Es" wound up the voyage. But the road still remains. The traveller has reached certain assumptions.

> asylum under my tread all this day
> their muffled revels as the flesh falls
> breaking without fear or favour wind
> the gantelope of sense and nonsense run
> taken by the maggots for what they are[68]

Death is shown as the point to which all things tend. The 'I' neither idealizes it nor finds it unacceptable. But death eludes him, as does peace. Line three of "Echo's Bones" is an echo from "Serena III." The steadily worked out rejection of all hopes in the other poems brings about this conclusion where even Art and the self become insignificant and only Death has 'being.'

Continued exposure to the poems in *Echo's Bones* is an exciting prospect. They swim more clearly into focus. Yet there is an element of instability in them because they were written at a time when Beckett was only evolving as an artist. The result is a bewildering kaleidoscopic panorama of and for the senses. The poems differ from the jettisoned ones primarily because they are a sequence and secondarily, owing to the fact that they do better what the others were attempts of. Thus the formless poems in the collection push formlessness to a more exciting degree (e.g., "Sanies II") than those like "Text." The lyrics are less sentimental, hence better. The best example is "Da Tagte Es." The organic unity of the sequence, everywhere evident, the scope for intellectualization that is fully exploited and the multiplicity of themes, references, images, sounds, smells and sights all play their part in making the collection as formidable a challenge to the reader as Pound's *Cantos,* Eliot's *The Waste Land* and some of the more complex poems to come out in recent years. But it must be stated that they still belong partially to Beckett's "years of learning." The mysteries are not yet "all of their own making."[69] Some of them are the result of technical ineptitude and others because of an approach to art that sometimes border on the unnecessarily obscure and harsh in sound or iconoclastic.

It may be pointed out that in using the alba as a form Beckett was representative of modernism, since interest in Provençal verse-forms was revived by poets like Ezra Pound and T.S. Eliot. Pound has written an alba in his collection *Lustra*. Eliot has written a nocturne. But in reviving the enueg and the planh and inventing the sanie, even as he revived the gnome and the xenien, Beckett has contributed to the forms available to English verse.

The unity of *Echo's Bones* is different from that of "Whoroscope." It has a more ambivalent nature. In the latter the links that hold the poem together seem more often than not reasoned or reasonable. In the collection it is different. The connections are not always rational. They seem more instinctive. 'Echo's Bones,' the title, for example, is connected to the word 'sanies' by the fact that sanies refer to the body's emissions and may hence be about Echo's physiological dehiscence into a voice. The connection has its basis in etymology and may have been intended as a logical extension by Beckett. In "Serena III" the last four lines read:

> so say your prayers now and go to bed
> your prayers before the lamps start to sing behind the larches
> here at these knees of stone
> then to bye-bye on the bones[70]

This is obviously a reference to the title. But the rationale is not so obvious. The semantic significance of the lines, while not completely elusive, can be connected with that of the title only tangentially. In the last poem the title appears again as a subtitle of the envoi to the collection. One feels that these links, while clearly intended to connect the poems, are organic and not meant to charge the poem with a cumulative revelation. This is the difference between Eliot's studied fitting together of fragments in his sequences *Ash Wednesday* and *Four Quartets* and Beckett's more haphazard method. His aims are different. In *Echo's Bones* he is trying out what he learned to do well later, i.e., to situate his writing between unity and chaos in the region of 'interface' that problematically eludes being named even by post-structuralists. Derrida's 'trace' or 'sign under erasure' comes closest. Beckett is partially successful in this attempt. Even in the case of the title the fact that it is referred to or seemingly evoked in different parts of the collection gives rise to a dual implication. On the one hand it unites or suggests unity. On the other, by not inhering very rationally into the sequence it suggests that poetry is not about structural perfection but an energy that flickers in its words and transcends the whole. *Echo's Bones* has this energy in spite of its many imperfections, so that even after knowing it was written by Beckett when he was only in his twenties, wandering, learning the ropes, it has its magnetism.

The range of forms and themes in the collection remains surprising. At the risk of repetition one enumerates. The lyric (i.e., the short poem), the dawn-song, the serenade, the nocturne, the enueg, the planh, the elegy, the poems of grief, woe and mourning, the travelogue, the picaresque narrative, prose, fiction, (auto-)biography, fantasy, bawdy, the lament, the tagelied, the quest, the voyage, the journey etc., are all forms implicated in Beckett's search for expression in the modern environment. The themes include love, sex, eroticism, women, voyeurism, sadism, masochism, the family, Art, God, Christ, solitude, exile, rejection, suffering, time, memory, the reach of the imagination, the awareness of the distinctiveness of places, the question of nationality, metamorphoses, metaphysics, psychology, deaths etc. Compression, elision and selection have made *Echo's Bones* the seed or germ of Beckett's later works where he is often seen as only enlarging on the hints in it. It has also made it a fertile excavatory-ground for critics for a long time to come.

Notes and References

1. M.L. Rosenthal and Sally Gall, The Modern Poetic Sequence (New York: O.U.P., 19)
2. Samuel Beckett, "The Vulture," *Collected Poems 1930-1978* (London: Calder, 1984) 9. All the subsequent quotations from Beckett's poems in this chapter are from this book.
3. René DesCartes, *A Discourse on Method* (London: Dent, 1984) 27
4. Berkeley in Samuel Beckett's "Film," *The Complete Dramatic Works* (London: Faber, 1986) 323.
5. Beckett, "Ill Seen Ill Said" *The New Yorker Magazine* (New York: 5 Oct. issue, 1981) 48-58.
6. Beckett, *Molloy* (London: Picador, 1979) 10.
7. Beckett, "Cascando," *The Complete Dramatic Works* (London: Faber, 1986) 700.
8. Beckett, *How It Is* (London: Calder & Boyars, 1964)1.
9. Beckett, "Enueg I," *C.P.* 10.
10. Ibid.
11. *The Concise Oxford English Dictionary* (India: O.U.P., 1985) 134
12. Beckett, "Enueg I," *C.P.* 10.
13. Beckett, "Dante and the Lobster," *More Pricks Than Kicks* (London: Calder & Boyars, 1970) 14-15.
14. Maria Jolas, *"Beckett at 60: A Festchrift*. ed. John Calder (London: Calder & Boyars, 1967) 16.
15. Beckett, *Molloy* (London: Picador, 1979) 26.
16. T.S. Eliot, Chorus 1, in "Choruses from The Rock," *Selected Poems* (London: Faber, 1924) 110.

17. Beckett, "Enueg I," *C.P.* 11.
18. Ibid.
19. Democritus in Samuel Beckett's *Murphy* (London: Picador, 1973) 138.
20. Beckett, "Enueg I," *C.P.*11
21. Ibid.
22. Matthew 18. 36, The Authorised King James Version of The Bible (London: T.B.S., 1990) 694
23. Beckett, "Enueg I," *C.P.* 11.
24. Ibid., 12.
25. Ibid.
26. Ibid.
27. Ibid.
28. Dante, "Inferno," *The Selected Works* (London: Chatto & Windus, 1972) 15.
29. The last stanza of "Enueg I" is based on Rimbaud's "Barbare." In the margin to the poem Rimbaud added a note: "Elles n' existent pas." They don't exist. As Perloff notes, Beckett skews the quotation ever so slightly, so that it becomes "That don't exist." The result, as she says, retains Rimbaud's poetic immediacy but rejects his "magic-lantern slide show." Lawrence E. Harvey, *Samuel Beckett* (New Jersey: Princeton U.P., 1970) 72-73 & Majorie Perloff, *The Poetics of Indeterminacy* (New Jersey: Princeton U.P., 1981) 228.
30. Beckett, "Enueg I," *C.P.* 12.
31. In 1931 Samuel Putnam, the co-editor of *The European Caravan*, published a blurb on Beckett's poems that says among other relevant things: "Samuel Beckett ... has a great knowledge of Romance Literature, is a friend of ... Joyce, and has adopted the Joyce method to his poetry with original results." This is true of many of Beckett's jettisoned poems and of some in *Echo's Bones. Samuel Beckett: His Works and His Critics, An Essay in Bibliography* eds. Federman & Fletcher (Berkeley: U.of California P., 1970) 10.
32. Beckett, "Enueg II," *C.P.* 13-14.
33. William Wordsworth, *The Golden Treasury*, ed. F.T.Palgrave (London: Dent, 1976) 311.
34. Hugh Kenner, *A Reader's Guide to Samuel Beckett* (London: Thames & Hudson, 1973) 44.
35. Ibid.
36. Harvey, *Samuel Beckett* 79.
37. Beckett, "Alba," *C.P.* 15.

38. Beckett, "Dortmunder," *C.P.* 16.
39. T.S. Eliot, "The Waste Land," *The Faber Book of Modern Verse*, ed. Michael Roberts, Peter Porter (London: Faber, 1982) 123.
40. Beckett, *Proust* (New York: Grove P., 1970) 66.
41. Ibid., 70
42. Harvey, *Samuel Beckett* 104.
43. Beckett, "Sanies I," *C.P.* 17.
44. Ibid.
45. Ibid., 18.
46. Ibid.
47. Beckett, "Fingal," *More Pricks Than Kicks* 31.
48. Beckett, "Sanies I," *C.P.* 17.
49. Ibid.
50. Beckett 17-18.
51. Ibid., 18.
52. Beckett, "Sanies II," *C.P.* 20.
53. Beckett, "Serena I," *C.P.* 21-22.
54. Ibid.
55. Ibid.
56. Beckett, "Sanies I," *C.P.* 17.
57. Beckett, "Serena II," *C.P.* 24.
58. Beckett, "Serena III," *C.P.* 25.
59. Ibid.
60. Beckett, "Ding Dong," *A Samuel Beckett Reader* (London: Picador, 1983) 46.
61. Beckett, "Serena III," *C.P.* 25.
62. Thom Gunn, "On the Move," *Selected Poems 1950-1975* (London: Faber, 1979) 16.
63. A.M. Toplady, "Rock of Ages Cleft for Me," *The Book of Common Prayer* (London: Fontana) 50.
64. Beckett, "Malacoda," *C.P.* 26.
65. Emily Dickinson, "Because I could not stop for Death," *American Literature 1890-1965* (India: Eurasia Publishers, 1967) 332.
66. Beckett, "Da Tagte Es," *C.P.* 27.
67. Beckett, "Echo's Bones," *C.P.* 28.
68. Ibid.
69. Beckett, *Disjecta* (London: Calder, 1983) 109.
70. Beckett, "Serena II," *C.P.* 24.

3

The Mature Phase: The Blue Celeste of Poesy

Beckettians get a glimpse of his ability to write short well-crafted poems that excel from reading "Yoke of Liberty," "Gnome," "The Vulture" and "Da Tagte Es." After 1935, although Beckett wrote poems only sporadically and they are but few in number, most of them are qualitatively as fine as or better than the poems just mentioned. On the whole, despite a few more instances of failure, Beckett emerged into maturity as a poet. He left behind him not only the flaws of his juvenilia but also the imitativeness and unwonted allusiveness of *Echo's Bones*. His later poems are usually both different and original in comparison with those of his contemporaries. They have a timbre that is all their own and an assurance of touch that ensures them a secure niche in the history of poetry. These poems, i.e., the ones among them that matter, can vie for the attention of not just Beckettians but all who are interested in fine poetry.

The first of these is "Cascando" (1936). It must not be confused with Beckett's radio-play of 1962. The two have nothing in common except the name. It was not unusual for Beckett to indulge in this sort of whimsy. The poem "Text" and the collection *Echo's Bones* both have prose parallels with the same name, but the content is quite dissimilar. "Malacoda" and the short story "Draff" have different names but the theme and even most of the details are the same. Beckett has always made full use of the freedom and infinite possibilities available to the writer in playing the game of literature. These are miniscule examples of this attitude. "Cascando" has a German version. Beckett was the translator. It is called "Mancando." Both the titles are taken from Western classical music. A cascando is "a musical direction indicating diminishing volume and decreasing tempo" and 'mancando' signifies "dying away."[1] The poem's form and content devolve accordingly.

CASCANDO

1

Why not merely the despaired of
occasion of
wordshed

is it not better abort than be barren

the hours after you are gone are so leaden
they will always start dragging too soon
the grapples clawing blindly the bed of want
bringing up the bones the old loves
sockets filled once with eyes like yours
all always is it better too soon than never
the black want splashing their faces
saying again nine days never floated the loved
nor nine months
nor nine lives

2

saying again
if you don't teach me I shall not learn
saying again there is a last
even of last times
last times of begging
last times of loving

of knowing not knowing pretending
a last even of last times of saying
if you do not love me I shall not be loved
if I do not love you I shall not love
the churn of stale words in the heart again
love love love thud of the old plunger
pestling the unalterable
whey of words

terrified again
of not loving
of loving and not you
of being loved and not by you
of knowing not knowing pretending
pretending
I and all the others that will love you
if they love you

3

unless they love you[2]

The poem's beginning approaches literary creation from a point of view that is different from the usual. It stresses the weakness of the process without suggesting that the attempt to create is nobly ambitious, unlike traditional invocations to the muse. It introduces writing as a form of de-creation. The neologism "wordshed" in line three, reminiscent of bloodshed, raises the idea that writing resembles an act of violence. Beckett's language in this poem, lyrical and deceptively simple, is an example of his ability to unleash irreconcilable contradictions in the same breath with seeming clarity. To try to unravel the implications of his lines is worthwhile because of the intriguing insights gained as a result. The first section, for example, implies that literature or writing is a futile exercise with the use of the word "merely." But it instantly annuls such an inference in its next few words that read "the despaired of occasion." This, besides suggesting that writing is a desperate act hints at writing as an imperative necessity, if one places emphasis on the word "occasion," that the writer half-hopes and half-fears may not take place. Beckett is an adept at saying several things that exist in antagonism to one another at the same time. This accounts for the tension his writing creates in the reader who finds it difficult to be faced with a surface that has "the power to claw"[3] and draws its strength from having "the potential for meaning while never permitting meaning to come to rest."[4] The next line in the poem that compares writing to abortion or sterility is similarly incisive and excisive. The absurdity is only superficial. Beckett is sensitive as an artist that to tarry long before writing may lead to what was meant to be written not being put down. He is also aware that to write may be to commit to paper what is premature or even stillborn, quality-wise. The writer is forced to choose, then to create, and hope that silence is not the better alternative.

After this initial or first 'movement' "Cascando" enters on its theme of "love." The lover describes the sorrow of separation. By converting the verb "grapples" into a noun in line seven, he creates a metaphor for the agony he goes through while his beloved is absent that is effective. In line eight absence is shown to be unendurable because it brings to the narrator's memory his previous affairs, and a haunting image of "sockets" from which the eyes of his "old loves," once full of life, have fled. There is a covert allusion for the sophisticated reader to spot here, to "bones", that refers to *Echo's Bones* as a record of failures in loving. It is interesting to notice because one sees how Beckett begins more and more confidently to grasp at intertextuality as a technical principle that will connect his works one with another. The result is a reverberation of repetitions that helps the texts gain in significance and effect. The poet wonders if parting, if inevitable, is better if undertaken quickly rather than never. The pretty paradox in such a line of thought that suggests more than it nullifies is precisely what is typical of Beckett. The poem which seems to be about love turns out, on a closer inspection, to be about the lack or absence of it. The narrator lacks love and he needs a partner to complete him. But it turns out that the same "want" or lust exists, or was passed on by him like "the black" (1. 11) plague to those he tried to love. The consistent note in Beckett is the negativeness of his vision, be it of life, art or whatever else. In the case of love too, even if it is only eroticism or pretense, he steadfastly insists that its lifespan cannot exceed even the nine days it takes a drowned corpse to surface. It does not have the cat's proverbial "nine lives." Nor can it survive as the baby does in the womb for "nine months." The uncertainty in the writing over the meaning of words spreads through the work to the preceding and the following lines. Is line four not only about literary creation but also on the love affair? It can be. May not one think of the first three lines in the context of what follows as a comparison of the writing-act to the acts of abortion and divorce? One may. The reader is kept guessing and every reading is finally the result of his personal predilections in the face of the text's indeterminacy.

The second part of the poem is an astonishing tour de force. The language wavers between that used in trite romance novels and extremely powerful metaphoric lines to depict the inner state of the disintegrating thwarted lover who is trying to stall a parting that seems more a certainty of the past than a thing of the future. The unforgettable imagery in lines twenty-five to twenty-eight, the poem's central stanza, suggests that the act of writing, the nature of love and the experience of sexual intercourse are similar, in a mixed metaphor that includes the nouns "plunger" and "heart" and the verb "pestling" and is the best part of second movement of this sonata-poem. The impossibility of the narrator's aspiration to love is covertly implied by the reference to "whey" which cannot be pestled and "words" which are "unalterable" and "stale" but without substitutes; faults which the poet tries to rectify helplessly. The heart being called "the old plunger" is a sly pun. The poet exposes the gap between authorial intention and expression but paradoxically produces arresting lines of verse in the process.

Beckett's entropic world is always running down but it never comes to a full stop. Thus, in "Cascando," the author speaks of "a last even of last times" but since the threat is preceded by the words "saying again" the end remains distant. Recurrence is implied by repetition. Similarly, there is a play in Beckett's text on absence and the possibility of presence that is deconstructive. Thus, in the penultimate line of the poem, Beckett posits love as an impossibility not only for himself but also for others, but in the last line, i.e., the postlude of this poem, he seems to say that it is not impossible for others. This constant double entendre keeps the reader on tenterhooks. The same uncertainty is applicable to a description of Beckett's language. It verges on the prosaic without losing out on being poetic. "Cascando" ends in accordance with the title, in a whimper. The repetitions in the poem, while not yet a part of his formal strategy, are noticeable since this is the first poem in which they play such a prominent part. It is an interesting detail for the reader to know that the first version of "Cascando" did not have the first three lines and the "not" in line four.

Beckett started writing in French in 1937. He soon brought out a collection of poems in French. It was titled "Poèmes 1937-'39." Two of them have English versions. They are "they come" and "Dieppe." "They come" was written in French and translated into English. "Dieppe" was translated from the English to French.

they come
different and the same
with each it is different and the same
with each the absence of love is different
with each the absence of love is the same.[5]

The poem extends Beckett's position on love. Love is defined via negativa, by its absence. That is to say it is not defined. One can infer that it cannot be defined or is inexpressible. Identity and universality are explored in the poem and shown to be binary opposites that cancel each other out with mathematical precision. But the 'logic' of poetry is also involved. Thus people are different from each other yet "the same." Their lack of love for one another or the narrator may differ in slight respects but amounts to being identical. The common factor is the absence of love or the presence of pretense. In this detached poem which is direct since the meaning is evident, our attention shifts to the form where repetition and variation plays the main part. Enumeration, and permutation and combination, in dialectics leads inevitably to the discovery that each concept that can be expressed verbally leads to the creation of its antinomy, its binary opposite and its duplicate. This is the Hegelian nature of language. In the poem, difference is understood in relation to a concept's binary opposite and its duplicate. Love, therefore, is understood not in relation to hate but the absence of love. The words "difference," "same," "absence" and "love" are entrenched in the mind of the reader by simple 'duplicity,' that is, mere repetition. This shows up the insufficiency of language. It cannot signify adequately. By a process which cannot be described in words, the difference between the singular and the plural is both affirmed and abolished in the poem. But the poem is not without a consistent rational framework. It is still grounded firmly in the Cartesian world of dualism where the self exists as a separate, observing entity and a subject that experiences, opposed to the world. This makes the narrator's impersonal voice a mask. The narrator is a spectator who is indirectly involved.

"Dieppe," the other translation in the collection, is based on a lyric by the German poet Hölderlin titled "Der Spaziergang."

> Dieppe
> again the last ebb
> the dead shingle
> the turning then the steps
> towards the lights of old.[6]

Dieppe is a town in France by the seaside. Beckett visited it during the war. The phrase in Hölderlin's poem which impressed Beckett deeply is "und dann der steg"[7] (and then the steps). Originally the last line in "Dieppe" read" towards the lighted town."[8] Beckett's favourite word, "again," starts the poem suggesting the ceaseless flux of life. The landscape of the beach, the space between land and sea, is an image that recurs continually in Beckett's works. For an artist seeking an 'objective correlative' in words for states between life and death, love and hate, sleep and waking, music and silence, withdrawal and engagement etc., such images come naturally. The tension between the needs for solitude and company is reflected in the poem and temporarily resolved, for once, against the self and for the world. The title may also suggest 'the ebb.' The idea of recurrence is again evoked. There is a touch of melancholy about the poem that gives it its lyrical quality. "Dieppe" reappears in prose in *Watt*[9] and is the germ of many passages in Beckett's later works.

In 1938 Beckett wrote "Ooftish," a Yiddish expression meaning "put your money down on the table."[10]

> Ooftish
> offer it up plank it down
> Golgotha was only the pot egg

cancer angina it is all one to us
cough up your T.B. don't be stingy
no trifle is too trifling not even a thrombus
anything venereal is especially welcome
that old toga in the mothballs
don't be sentimental you won't be wanting it again
send it along we'll put it in the pot with the rest
with your love requited and unrequited
the things taken too late the things taken too soon
the spirit aching bullock's scrotum
you won't cure it you won't endure it
it is you it equals you any fool has to pity you
so parcel up the whole issue and send it along
the whole misery diagnosed undiagnosed misdiagnosed
get your friends to do the same we'll make use of it
we'll make sense of it we'll put it in the pot with the rest
it all boils down to blood of lamb.[11]

The poem is obscure because one cannot ascertain who the "we" and the "you" in it are. The "we" may refer to the tormentors who appear regularly in Beckett's fictions with names like Bim, Pim, Bom etc. The "you" then become (s) the tortured. The poem is once again in the form of an enueg, listing as it does the great and small vexations of life. Beckett extends sympathy to Jesus Christ who as the Son of Man suffered on the cross at Golgotha. He considers that death as symbolic of all the suffering each man and the human race has to go through. But Beckett does not see suffering as either sacrificial or redemptive. He does not offer spiritual insight into the value of suffering or its necessary place in life. So his reaction is bitter. It extends pity to those who suffer but does not penetrate beyond the veil of appearances to understand suffering as part of any divine pattern whereby either the refinement of character or justice is made possible.

During the Second World War, Beckett was mostly busy writing *Watt*. This sprawling anti-novel with its anti-hero, perhaps the first post-modern novel in English, was completed by 1945 but published only by 1953. *Watt* has in it four poems and four songs. The first, "To Nelly" (p. 11-12), is pornography put in prosody that is archaic. The result is hilarious, to say the least. The second poem experiments at a superficial level with repetition and variation and permutation and combination, without being bothered by the need for meaning. In spite of such an approach its last two lines are remarkable. The poem is as follows:

> We shall be here all night
> Be here all night shall we
> All night we shall be here
> Here all night we shall be
> One dark, one still, one breath
> Night here, here we, we night
> One fleeing, fleeing to rest
> One resting on the flight[12]

Lines two, three and four are amusing, but irrelevant. Lines five and six end in syntactical units that arise from the implicit laws of permutation and combination but are nonsensical. The last two lines, however, typify the two kinds of 'seekers' in the world effectively.

In the addenda to Watt, a poem that briefly describes the novel can be found. As an example that repetition and variation / permutation and combination could be incorporated into a powerful formal strategy, it may be the first of its kind in Beckett's works. The plays like Play (pub. 1964) and "Come and Go" (pub. 1967) have used this form well. The genesis of such a possibility is perhaps this poem. The content of the poem holds no interest apart from the novel but its form is what Beckett refines in his later poems, "Roundelay" and "thither." The line, the circle and the gyre are forms united in this poem into an unbroken continuity that is impressive. Beckett had tried this in "Calvary by Night," but this is done better. It shows that structural perfection was within Beckett's reach and his works experiment with 'open-ended' forms on purpose and not because he could not master various, closed traditional structures. The poem reads:

> Watt will not
> abate one jot
> but of what
>
> of the coming to
> of the being at
> of the going from
> Knott's habitat
> of the long way
> of the short stay
> of the going back home
> the way he had come
> of the empty heart
> of the empty hands
> of the dim mind wayfaring
> through barren lands
>
> of a flame with dark winds
> hedge about
> going out
> gone out
>
> of the empty heart
> of the empty hands
> of the dark mind stumbling
> through barren lands
>
> that is of what
> Watt will not
> abate one tot[13]

The poem begins with a question. The next six stanzas are the answer. Even for a reader unaware of the content of *Watt* the poem may stand in as a suitable substitute for the explanation that it is about the quest for Nothing that results in a parallel emptiness on the seeker's part. The puns on 'what' and 'not' are the obvious clues to this reading.

The four songs in *Watt*, two of which are the results of his schizophrenic nature, have interesting lyrics. The first is about a Magrew (34-35) whose youth, middle-age, aging and old age are all compared to the blooming, wilting, drooping and withering of a flower. The second stanza of the song is about how the life of man is meaningless and ends in death. It is an ironic song about the cycle of life which is actually death-oriented. In the figure of Magrew one has an early version of many of Beckett's woman characters like the Maddie Rooney of *All That Fall* and Winnie of *Happy Days*.

The second song in *Watt* (137-38) is the song of the frogs. Three frogs sing in croaks. They sound different and sound at different times but Beckett skilfully orchestrates their cries, sequencing them so that they start together, work out all the possible combinations and end simultaneously. Imposing order on chaos using a simple mathematical equation of progression, Beckett reveals himself as an avant-garde poet who could extend the frontiers of the possible forms of modern verse if he so wished.

The third song in *Watt* is a joke that draws on mathematics and wit of the type that endeared Lewis Carroll to children. One cannot be sure if Beckett is the author or not. The first three lines of the song are to be sung thrice.

> Said the column of cubes
> to the column of roots,
> "Oh what will you have to drink?"
> Said the column of roots
> to the column of cubes,
> "I'll have a bottle of ink."[14]

The fourth, in the addenda, is again one of the 'threnes' sung to Watt by the choir he hears in his head due to his schizophrenia. The words of the soprano are jumbled. She sings: "With all our heart breathe head awhile darkly apart the air exile of ended smile of ending care darkly awhile the exile air."[15] As Beckett's character in "What Where "says" make sense who may."[16] This short 'poem' speaks a lot to Beckettians of his life, philosophy and exile and of his plays like "Come and Go" but may not communicate to others.

In the addenda to *Watt* at the end of the novel a poem appears that both Beckett and his critics considered significant.

who may tell the tale
of the old man?
weigh absence in a scale?
mete want with a span?
the sum assess
of the world's woes?
nothingness
in words enclose?[17]

That Beckett thought this poem special can be seen by the fact that he opted to use it again as a 'tailpiece' to his *Collected Poems 1930-1978*. The foreword states: "This edition contains . . . a poem . . . added to Addenda (I) in the novel *Watt* . . . the author now thinks suitable as an 'Envoi' . . . "[18] A shift in emphasis occurred between the first appearance of the poem and its use as a tailpiece. In the former instance, though put in the interrogative form, it is declarative. Harvey says it is an "explicit statement of Beckett's plans as a writer."[19] It implies Beckett's 'I just may.' He launched out on writing his memorable works that deal with geriatric experiences, metaphysical concepts like Being, the awareness of "lessness," suffering and his attempt to express "the void" in language, after he marked out the path to be trod in this poem. *Molloy* etc., stems from this vision of what he had to do being pursued rigorously. But by the time the same poem appears as "Tailpiece" it epitomizes a different spirit, suggesting 'not even I can.' It is a confession of failure. In this second context the poem has become purely interrogative and reminds one of its original source, missed by many Beckettians. *Isaiah* 40. 12 reads: "Who has measured the waters in the hollow of his hand, and meted out heaven with the span, and comprehended the dust of the earth in a measure, and weighed the mountains in scales and the hills in a balance."[20] The answer remains the same then and now. God alone masters the impossible. But one can pause to survey the 'magnitude' of Beckett's failure. It stems from going in the opposite direction and has a certain admirable metaphysical vastness.

In 1946 Beckett wrote "Saint-Lô." It is a town in France where Beckett worked for a while after the war as an interpreter for the Red Cross. It was bombed during the war and reduced to rubble.

SAINT-LÔ

Vire will wind in other shadows
unborn through the bright ways tremble
and the old-mind ghost forsaken
sink into its havoc[21]

Vire is a river running through the town of St-Lô. The poet suggests that in the future the town will be rebuilt and as the river flows by, shadows of people and buildings will again fall on it. The latter couplet compares the state of St-Lô to the narrator's. Both, at present, seem to be inhabited by shadows or ghosts. But for St-Lô the exorcism of the ghosts of those who died in the war by the activity of restoration is a positive happening. It is not so for the narrator. He fears the eviction of the ghosts — memories that haunt him of his dead perhaps — from his mind since he feels it will then have no choice but to collapse as St-Lô did when the bombs exploded in it, into its primeval state of chaos.

In "First Love" (pub. 1977) a couplet appears that the narrator has prepared beforehand to be inscribed on his tomb. It renders in brief Beckett's view of life, humorously, in the form of an epitaph: "Hereunder lies the above who up below / so hourly died that he lived on till now."[22] Pozzo says in Waiting for Godot: "They give birth astride of a grave. The light gleams an instant, then it is gone."[23] In Beckett's dialectical use of language, his comments on life are also on death. The inseparability of the two is made clear. So is man's transience. The only things permanent in Beckett's world are change and his ability to state his mocking awareness of the emptiness of the lives of most men.

1949 saw the publication of "Poèmes 1947-'49." The collection contains six poems. Beckett translated three of them into English. They are the finest specimens available of Beckett's ability to write lyrics. Beckett's translation of Apollinaire's "Zone" was published in 1950. Besides being an excellent version it gives us the clue as to where Beckett got the pattern Jazz uses, that of the freefall, for his longer picaresque poems in *Echo's Bones*. Beckett's poems on wanderlust do not have the same gracefulness his translation of Apollinaire's famous poem has. But his lyrics in the six poems are a different proposition. They not only resemble Paul Eluard's that Beckett himself had translated superbly once in their mastery of the form but rivals them. This is obvious to the reader who reads both Beckett's translations of Eluard and his own mature short lyrics. Beckett was able to assimilate the influence of surrealism to the point where he could write poems extending the mode and also improve upon the scope of the lyric. His contribution is that the lyric was converted in his hands into an impersonal aesthetic vehicle to record emotions.

The metaphysical underpinning of Cartesianism, refined, extended and partially deconstructed helped him do this. The lyric is based on 'a priori' assumptions that the self and the world exist. Beckett re-introduces the Cartesian first principle of doubt. The result, when applied to the lyric, is a fluid morass where the self is no longer distinct but chimerical, the world even more so and the relationship between the two, based on unsure interpretations, partially illusory and kaleidoscopic. It is no wonder that the pervasive atmosphere in Beckett's mature poems is that of beauty caught in instability. The first translated lyric goes like this:

> my way is in the sand flowing
> between the shingle and the dune
> the summer rain rains on my life
> on me my life harrying fleeing
> to its beginning to its end
> my peace is there in the receding mist
> when I may cease from treading these long shifting thresholds
> and live the space of a door
> that opens and shuts[24]

The absence of punctuation-marks, capital letters (except for the 'I') and the fact that the grammatical structure of the sentence is replaced by the presence of lines and short phrasal units that may not make sense helps the poem achieve the ineffable. The images, the soft sibilant sounds, be they euphonic or alliterative, and the freshness of the unexpected connections ease the reader into a world where his seeing is altered into an awareness of the solitude of the self. Only the best poetry can induce such 'seeing.' As in "Dieppe," the images hint at the experience of in-betweenness. One cannot approach this category of poetry, modern and sensitive, by hunting for exact meanings. It can be appreciated only by verbalizing its balance between structure and formlessness in recognizable metaphors. The study of the links or adhesiveness between the images, beautiful, spontaneous and yet steadily creating the poem in the reader's mind as they weave and as lines progress is the ideal clue to unlocking these fragile poems' secrets. In the above poem, for example, the sands' mobility as a metaphor for the narrator's "way" teases the reader's mind into remembering the hour-glass (time) and quicksand (dying). "Summer" may stand for the second stage of life. Rain is unusual in summer. The autobiographical context helps if used judiciously. Beckett was in the summer of his life and career when he wrote these poems. Rain may suggest his creative fecundity then, for which he had to pay the prize of being divorced from external reality so that he could tread, in awful and awesome solitude, "the long shifting thresholds" that account for the depth in his art of the forties. But the narrator longs for unavailable "peace" that only death or utter simplicity that is ineluctable like the inscrutable image of "the space of a door/that opens and shuts" can give.

The second poem on the self from "Poèmes 1947-'49" that deals more rigorously with the inner world is perhaps more powerful.

> What would I do without this world faceless incurious
> where to be lasts but an instant where every instant
> spills in the void the ignorance of having been
> without this wave where in the end
> body and shadow together are engulfed
> what would I do without this silence where the murmurs die
> the pantings the frenzies towards succour towards love
> without this sky that soars above its ballast dust
>
> what would I do what I did yesterday and the day before
> peering out of my deadlight looking for another
> wandering like me far from all the living
> in a convulsive space
> among the voices voiceless
> that throng my hiddenness[25]

Its structure is breathtakingly simple. A question is asked and an incomplete answer is given, as in "Watt will not." In the first stanza, the "world" undergoes a series of transformations. It becomes "this wave," this silence" and "this sky." Each metamorphosis is relevant because it gives the impression that the poem has an impetus all its own that is leading it on inevitably towards its end. Meaning is absent but hyperactive in the lines. The reader's perception begins to waver as to who narrates. Is it Beckett, "the unnamable," oneself or the voice of every human being individualized and universalized to a nameless but recognizable degree. Does it belong to that elusive being called the real self that the ego is supposed to be only the surface of? If so, this deeper self is exposed as one that is unutterably lonely. It is not alive in the normal sense of the word. Beckett uses a rare word, "deadlight," to hint at this. But its solitude and invisibility are shared by the presence of "voices voiceless." Schizophrenia or an aesthetic experience that resembles semi-mystical revelation are both possible explanations of such a phenomenon. Being, existence, nothingness, the self, the world and solitude are metaphysical concepts glimpsed in the poem. The fortitude of the observer who is detachedly reporting a state of being that is by no means enviable lucidly is what infuses the poem with its maturity. If this distancing was not there Beckett's world would only have been merely unendurable, since it is made up of his private nightmares. The starkness of the solitude prevalent in the Beckettian landscape would strike one as terrifying if one was not made aware by the poet's cool tone that it is heightened to the point of obsession only to wring from it its aesthetic reality.

The last translated poem in the collection, about love for a change, harks back to "Cascando" and "they come." It shows that Beckett's attitude to love became progressively ruthless. His expression of it is refined hereto a pitch that intensifies this.

I would like my love to die
and the rain to be raining on the graveyard
and on me walking the streets
mourning her who thought she loved me[26]

The last line of the poem originally read "mourning the first and last to love me."[27] An interim version changed this line to "mourning her who sought to love me."[28] The final version, quoted above, seems quite the bleakest. The first line with its death-wish for another and the second where sorrow is ascribed to nature rather than to the self brings home to the reader in chilling terms the intricacies of human relationships. Does "my love" mean that I love or that I am loved? Either way, why the latter part of the line that reveals the desire for the death of the beloved? Is the death-wish beneficent or evil? Can rain be a substitute for tears? In the line four, is mourning a rite performed by the sky or the "I"? The poem's achievement lies in undermining the reader's ability to reach definite conclusions. Its imaginative skill is present in the fact that the last three lines propel one into a world where the first line is almost forgotten. But another shock awaits the reader in the "thought" of the last line. Beckett suggests that love, for most people, may be only selfishness or possessiveness. Using the phrase "walking the streets" is an aesthetic blunder on the part of the author because, for once, it shows him as being unaware of certain rules a sensitive poet should opt for if unnecessary meanings should not creep into his work. Here, the phrase may make the reader doubt the gender of the narrator without sufficient reason, and spoil the poem by causing a false reading resultantly.

Beckett's radio-play "Words and Music" of 1962, in which Words is one of the characters, contains two poems. The poems are about Age and Death respectively. Ideal examples of the lyric, they need little explanation.

SONG

Age is when to a man
Huddled over the ingle
Shivering for the hag
To put the pan in the bed
And bring the toddy
She comes in the ashes
Who loved could not be won
Or won not loved
Or some other trouble
Comes in the ashes
Like in that old light
The face in the ashes
That old starlight
On the earth again.[29]

The poem attempts, in miniature, to "tell the tale of" an "old man." Age is defined as the time when, married, ill, cold, waiting to be warmed by the fire in the hearth (ingle) and by alcohol (toddy), unable even to defecate without help, a man is suddenly haunted by the memory of the face of a woman he loved but could not win. The balance between emotion and impersonality with slight touches of beauty and poignancy is well struck. The use of the word "ingle" betrays Beckett's Irish origin. The poem shows the kind of simplicity one expects of the early Yeats. It is unfortunate that much of the time Beckett fought this tendency in himself and hence has left us with only a handful of much poems that are of this sort that can be included in the mainstream of English literature. As a rule, his poems belong to that marginal discourse that ensures his critics will be either scholars and Beckettians or intellectual litterateurs like Derrida, not the ordinary lover of poetry whose knowledge or preference is limited to songs and lyrics like the ones found in Palgrave's *Golden Treasury*.

The second poem in "Words and Music" is as follows:

Then down a little way
Through the trash
Towards where
All dark no begging
No giving no words
No sense no need
Through the scum
Down a little way
To whence once glimpse
Of that wellhead.[30]

The poem starts of as if it is describing the moment of birth, but actually it is the moment of dying that is pictured. Beckett equates the state of death to what Buddhists would describe as Nirvana in lines four to six since it can only be spoken of not in terms of identity but via negativa.

In 1947 Beckett returned to writing verse. His poems from then on, sometimes called poems only because he calls them so, are difficult to analyse. He wrote "dread nay" first. It can easily be recognized as a part of Beckett's work from "Imagination Dead Imagine" that deals with his version of the Biblical and Dantescan hells. Horror and science fiction also seem to be influences.

dread nay
head fast
in out as dead
till rending
long still
faint stir
unseal the eye
till still again
seal again

head sphere
ashen smooth

one eye
no hint when to
then glare
cyclop no
one side
eerily

on face
of outspread
vast in
the highmost
snow white
sheeting all
asylum head
sole blot

faster than where
in hellice eyes
stream till
frozen to
jaws rail
gnaw gnash
teeth with stork
clack chatter

come through
no sense and gone
while eye
shocked wide
with white
still to bare
stir dread
nay to nought

sudden in
ashen smooth
aghast
glittering rent
till sudden
smooth again

stir so past
never been

at ray
in latibule
long dark
stir of dread
till breach
long sealed
dark again
still again

so ere
long still
long nought
rent so
so stir
long past
head fast
in out as dead.[31]

The title defies explanation. It may be asking the reader to "dread" the experience of "nay." Or does it imply the poem is a description of "dread" nothing (-ness)? It can be that both these nuances are intended. The whole fantasy is hellish. The first four stanzas are clear. The first describes a head that looks as if it is dead inside and outside because it has been still for a long time. But this illusion is dispelled by the fact that it opens its eye and shuts it. The head is spherical and smooth. Its colour is pale, implied by the inclusion of the word "ashen" in its description. It has only one eye, not because it belongs to the race of Cyclops, those fabled giants whose sole eye was set in their forehead, but because the viewer, narrator or creator of this strange scene that slowly emerges before the reader's 'eyes' is seeing the face in perfect profile. This angle of vision gives the head its eerie look. The head is situated on the surface of the "outspread| vast in| the highmost" place. It is "snow white" all over in that place. The snow lies like a sheet over everything. Beckett calls the place or the head "asylum," paradoxically. In this landscape which perfectly symbolizes Nothingness, the head alone sticks out. Like the narrator of "The Unnamable" (1948) and "Texts for Nothing" (1949) the head weeps. Its tears turn to ice in the cold. Its weeping is more uncontrollable than that of those who weep, rail with their jaws and gnaw and gnash their teeth, with clacks that chatter as loudly as the beaks of storks, in hell. This reaction may be out of pain or because of the cold. The reference is to Jesus Christ's statement that for those who are left out of the Kingdom of God "there shall be weeping and gnashing of teeth."[32]

In the fifth stanza the poem loses its explicability. The reader is made to "come through no sense and go. . . " It is as if to portray an area of the imagination unknown to human experience as yet, Beckett has to alternate between clarity and a language of fragments that purposely refuse to signify or refer so that the reader may get a glimpse for himself of the state of such an existence. If Beckett is actually trying to portray Nothing in words perhaps this approach of incompleteness, uncertainty and "voices voiceless" is justifiable.

In stanza six the poem regains its simplicity. It repeats the content of stanza one. But in the seventh stanza a shift in perception occurs that, while easily noticeable, can again bewilder the reader. The head remains but the scene seems to have shifted. The description seems from within the head. The "snow white / sheeting all" has vanished. The reason for the head stirring and its dread, one discovers, is that a ray of light entered it or the "latibule" through a breach or the eye. It is sealed and all be comes dark again. Then "still" is restored for the head. The head returns to being "in out as dead." That the pun 'still' when used in such a context indicates both peace and death is an example of how Beckett toys with the reader's notions of the normal.

The head in the poem seems to have an independent life of its own that leads it to say no to being perceived, to light, and to dread any stir of returning to life. It seems another metaphor for Beckett's inner self that is hidden by the ego. But this inner self seems hardly enviable. Its citizenship is in that place described in *Genesis*, as "without form . . . void (chaos). . . darkness upon the face of the deep . . . the waters (confusion)."[33]

"Something there," also written in 1974, explores the same area of the imagination that "dread nay," "Lessness," "Ping," etc., does.

SOMETHING THERE

Something there
where
out there
out where
outside
what
the head what else
something there somewhere outside
the head

at the faint sound so brief
it is gone and the whole globe
not yet bare
the eye
opens wide
wide
till in the end
nothing more
shutters it again

so the odd time
out there

somewhere out there
like as if
as if
something
not life
necessarily[34]

As in "dread nay," "the head" and "the eye" hold the centrestage of the poem. In "Something there" also the ambiguity is created by a difficult stanza. Beckett's use of words or syntactical units in such a way that they relate to both the lines that precede and follow also causes difficulty. Thus in the first stanza, the "something there" may be either outside the head or a head outside. It is difficult to decide because the lineation is so done that it can be read first one way and then the other. Both readings will produce results consistent with the reader's choice. If one says that the 'something there' is outside the head the poem becomes a description by the head of an experience it had that cannot be verbalized adequately. The second stanza of the poem has in its gaps that are inexplicable.The line "the whole globe/not yet bare" cannot be explained. The eye, unlike in "dread nay," opens fully. The same infernal quality that exists in "dread nay" is introduced at the end of the poem by the words "not life / necessarily." Both "dread nay" and "Something there" seem connected to the Unnamable's head and the character called Worm in that book who is mainly an eye.

Traditional questions and answers seem irrelevant while dealing with such poetry. One cannot be impertinent enough as to ask who the narrator is. All the familiar landmarks in ordinary discourse like gender, nationality, time, place, religion, the rules of language, human relationships etc., are erased. Even the self is no longer whole, though solitary. It is dismembered. The voice is impersonal and may belong to one unborn, alive, dead or from the after-life. But the aesthetic tension remains unabated. The reader is apparently brought to realizations that go beyond the surface of appearances, about the fragility of language, the instability of the self, the indecipherability of the object and the invalidity of the vague relationship between the two. His expectations are capsized. The result is, surprisingly enough, enervating and illuminating at the same time.

One hears the dying voice of an individual stripped of even the necessary vestiges of impositions who in the midst of such an experience of the imagination retains enough lucidity to try to find an adequately (in-)sane form for it. Beckett is able to move in Nothing without being overpowered by its traumatic qualitylessness.

The poems "Roundelay" and "thither" of 1976 move onto cover new ground. They make use of repetition and variation, reminiscent of Gertrude Stein's pieces like "A Very Valentine" and achieve musical smoothness. A roundelay is "a simple, short song with a refrain."[35] The landscape in "Roundelay" harks back to "Dieppe" and the radio-play *Embers* (1959) and forwards to a fragment of *Company* (1982).

Roundelay
On all that strand
at end of day
steps sole sound
until unbidden stay
then no sound
on all that strand
long no sound
until unbidden go
steps sole sound
long sole sound
on all that strand
at end of day.[36]

Random steps on the beach that pace, rest, then pace again, restless, are evoked with precision through image and repetition to offer a powerful metonym for solitude. The sound of the "footfalls" is onomatopoeically maintained in the poem's choice of rhythm, words and the length of the lines. A measured tread can be heard in them. One may wonder why this particular landscape has such fascination for Beckett. The sea is one of his symbols for death. It contains the dead. He visits the strand so often, signifying the pull of death and the reluctance of the self to die. In "Dieppe," while young, the strand-walk resulted in a decision for life, against death. In *Embers*, the sea's symbolic aspect is explained. Henry sits on the strand, but never goes into the sea to swim because his father drowned there.[37] It again suggests Beckett's rejection of death. "Roundelay" is poised between rejection and acceptance. Age may be the factor responsible for this. In *Company* the strand appears for the last time and the old man in it is shown standing still, his back to the sea, finally aware that he has to die whether he comes to terms with Death's reality or not.[38] This is the logical conclusion to this constant motif in Beckett's works that evolved over the years and appears even in "my way is in the sand. . . " and *Molloy*. In reviving the roundelay as a form, Beckett shows that his interest in archaic forms never died out. No one has written a roundelay in recent times except Beckett. The technique of repetition and variation that started to appear in "they come" and continued in the two poems in *Watt* reaches its peak here and in "thither."

"Thither" reminds us, surprisingly enough, of William Wordsworth because 'daffodils' are mentioned in it.

THITHER

thither
a far cry
for one
so little
fair daffodils
march then

then there
then there
then thence
daffodils
again
march then
again
a far cry
again
for one
so little[39]

The use of archaic expressions and words like "thither," "thence" and "a far cry" gives the poem the feel of an English lyric of the Romantic or Victorian age. The poem is simple but lacks sentimentality. This gives it its strength. The child's — if child it be[40] — situation is not idealized. The rhythm of plodding is captured perfectly in the second stanza. Those who have listened to minimalist music by composers like Philip Glass[41] will readily admit that Beckett's is a literary parallel to such minimalism. They may also grant him recognition as a modern Irish master of the lyric.

"Neither," published in 1979, is a metaphysical poem. It shows how Beckett never got over DesCartes' influence, though he has subverted his position.

NEITHER

to and fro in shadow from inner to outer shadow
from impenetrable self to impenetrable unself
by way of neither

as between two lit refuges whose doors once
gently close, once turned away from
gently part again
beckoned back and forth and turned away
heedless of the way, intent on the one gleam
or the other

unheard footfalls only sound

till at last halt for good, absent for good
from self and other

then no sound
then gently light unfading on that unheeded
neither

unspeakable home[42]

The first stanza (esp., lines two and three) explains the state of existence. The second stanza makes this clear with the use of an extended simile. It is a simile for a metaphor of an inexplicable reality that the poet wishes to verbalize. The poem develops the situation of a pendulum-like movement within a "closed space."[43] Then the movement is stilled. The narrator, the perceiver of a perceiver who is attempting to perceive the imperceptible, states unequivocally that while the self, the world ("the impenetrable unself") and the self trying to perceive itself cannot be known, the "neither" inhabited by the self trying to perceive itself may be verbalized metaphorically with the use of the prefix 'un.' One cannot ascertain whether the poem is the result of too much of speculative philosophy on the part of the author or linguistic complexity that multiplies terms in the very process of trying to simplify the essential. Howbeit, "neither" is substantially simple, expressive and even communicative of Beckett's ontological anxiety that he appeases temporarily by his ability to express his inexpressiveness so well. To attain such negative clarity is a task no one has either attempted or succeeded in before. Beckett proves his mastery of the language and the depth of the certainty in him as to his vision. "Neither" is a poem a philosopher, an artist and the Eastern mystic who feels that the self is quality-less may all relish.

In 1981, Beckett published a three-poem sequence that he called "croaks." The last of his English poems, one fragment of this sequence, aptly titled "PPS" (post-postscriptum) appears in Nicholas Zurbrugg's essay "Ill Seen Ill Said and the Sense of an Ending."

> head oh hands
> hold me
> unclasp
> hold me[44]

Like Paola Zaccaria's interpretation of a section of "Still" (1973) one is tempted to say that the poem refers to thinking and writing and "he makes the head-the place of thoughts, memories, where writing was born-touch the hand, the agent of writing."[45] What strikes the present reader about "PPS" is how by using simple words, the absence of capital letters and punctuations and sensitive lineation Beckett creates multiplicity; innumerable potential meanings that await readers. In Beckett's case it may be partially true that there are as many meanings to his poems as there are readers. He has discovered and exposed the transparence and translucence of language that signifies and impedes signification, referring to and veiling the signified's in-significance, significantly. Irrespective of the variance a reader may feel at with Beckett in the matter of content he cannot but admire his resourcefulness, inventiveness and originality in the matter of forms and structures. By always changing these, he remains fresh with each attempt. The poems studied in this chapter may seem failures in sensitivity to a reader used to poets[46] like G.M. Hopkins, St. John of the Cross, Eliot etc., who explore the mystery of language and are able to write from within and without it so as to affect the reader positively, but they are not. Beckett refrains from coercing the reader into taking a stance for or against his dialectical forms. His art eludes the question of how to come to terms with life and hence even his best poems concentrate only on deepening one's awareness of the contrary natures language has. In this, however, he excels. This may be Beckett's significant, most authentic contribution.

Notes and References

1. Samuel Beckett, "Lessness," *A Samuel Beckett Reader*. ed. John Calder (London: Picador, 1983) 262.
2. Lawrence E. Harvey, *Samuel Beckett: Poet and Critic* (New Jersey: Princeton U.P.,1970) 174.
3. Beckett, "Cascando," *Collected Poems 1930-1978* (London: Calder, 1984) 29-30.
4. Stephen Barker, "Conspicuous Absence: Trace and Power in Beckett's Drama," *Rethinking Beckett*, ed. Lance St. John Butler and Robin J. Davis (London: Macmillan, 1990) 186
5. Beckett, "they come," *C.P.* 41.
6. Beckett, "Dieppe," *C.P.* 51.
7. Harvey, *Samuel Beckett* 218.
8. Ibid., 219.
9. Beckett, *Watt* (New York: Grove P., 1970) 40. "... on the dark shingle the turning for the last time again to the lights of the little town . . ."It occurs in Arsene's monologue to Watt. All subsequent quotations from *Watt* in the chapter are from this Grove Press edition.
10. Harvey, *Samuel Beckett* 156.
11. Beckett, "Ooftish", *C.P.* 31, 174
12. Beckett, *Watt* 47.
13. Ibid., 249-50.
14. Ibid., *Watt* 193.
15. Ibid., *Watt* 253.
16. Beckett, "What Where," *The Complete Dramatic Works* (London: Faber, 1986) 476.
17. Beckett, *Watt* 247.
18. John Calder, "Foreword" in Samuel Beckett's *C.P.* ix.
19. Harvey, *Samuel Beckett* 400.
20. Isaiah 40.12, *The Authorised Version of the King James Bible* (London: T.B.S., 1990) 682.
21. Beckett, "Saint-Lô" *C.P.* 32.
22. Beckett, *"First Love," A Samuel Beckett Reader* 87.

23. Beckett, *Waiting for Godot* (London: Faber, 1951).
24. Beckett, "my way is in the sand . . .," *C.P.* 59.
25. Beckett, "what would I do . . .," *C.P.* 61.
26. Beckett, "I would like . . .," *C.P.* 63.
27. John Calder, in Beckett's *C.P.* 176.
28. Ibid
29. Beckett, "Song," *C.P.* 37
30. Beckett, "Words and Music," *The Complete Dramatic Works* 293-94.
31. Beckett, "dread nay," *C.P.* 33-35.
32. Jesus Christ, Matthew 24. 16, *The Authorised Version of the King James* Bible 913.
33. Moses, Genesis 1.2, (partially) *The Authorised Version of the King James Bible* 5.
34. Beckett, "Something there," *C.P.* 65
35. *The Concise Oxford Dictionary* 1982. (Bombay: O.U.P., 1985) 910
36. Beckett, "Roundelay," *C.P.* 35.
37. Beckett, "Embers," *The Complete Dramatic Works* 254. Henry: "I'm like you [his father] in that, can't stay away from it [the sea] but I never go in, no ..."
38. Beckett, *Company* (London: Calder, 1980) 75. "A strand. Evening. Light dying. Soon none left to die. No. No such thing then as no light. Died on to dawn and never died. You stand with your back to the wash. No sound flows again. You lean on a long staff. Your hands rest ..."
39. Beckett, "thither," *C.P.* 36.
40. The "little one" in "thither" need not be a child because in "Lessness" Beckett introduces a 'being' who has a "little heart body." But it may also be a child. Ref. Beckett's "Lessness," *A Samuel Beckett Reader* 259
41. Philip Glass's overture, the title-track, in his *Quoyanisquatsi* comes especially to mind.
42. Beckett, "neither," *Journal of Beckett Studies 4* (London: Calder, Spring 1979).
43. Beckett, "Closed Place," *Collected Shorter Prose 1945-1980* (London: Calder, 1984) 199
44. Nicholas Zurbrugg, "Ill Seen Ill Said and the Sense of an Ending," *Beckett's Later Fiction and Drama: Texts for Company*, ed. James Acheson and Kateryna Arthur (New York: St. Martin's P., 1987) 155, 58.
45. Paola Zaccaria, "Fizzles by Samuel Beckett: The Failure of the Dream of a Never-ending Verticality," Rethinking Beckett 115.
46. The word 'poet' is used in the sentence in the Aristotelian sense of 'one who creates with his words.'

Conclusion: Transcendng the Roots of Resistance in Language

It seems necessary at the end of this study of Samuel Beckett's poems in English to briefly sum up their salient features and to state their original contribution to the discourse of poetry. The poetic devices Beckett used, the forms he employed, the structures involved and the semantic complexities evoked demand such an unravelling. Enumeration of this sort, if exhaustive, can also be exhausting and repetitions cannot be entirely avoided. But the effort is not without gain because light can be shed on what is actually memorable about Beckett's few English poems.

In the introduction to this book it was stated that Beckett's poems could be broadly categorized as belonging to two periods. They are his early and mature phases. In the early phase he started out as an imitative poet. He developed into being not only representative and typical of modernism but also impatiently desirous of advancing beyond it. These years have hence been called, with the help of an appropriate quote from his poem "Gnome," those of learning and wandering. They are the years in which he produced the jettisoned poems and *Echo's Bones*. Biographically speaking too, they were years of study and travelling. But the poems of the second phase are different. They are usually mature and hence that period has been named "the blue celeste of poesy." When one looks at the poetic devices or contrivances which Beckett constantly used during these two periods, it is possible to see some as belonging only to the first period while some are of the second. A few techniques appear in both phases. To point these out with their applications, in miniscule, may help broaden our understanding of Beckett's aesthetics regarding poetry and his ability to execute the same. They also illustrate the changes that came over his writing, showing that he was not static creatively.

Poetic Devices

A. Titling

A poem can exist with or without a title. The traditional approach is to have or give one. But the moderns have found that titles can be experimental or omitted. Beckett has used these three options in his poems. Beckett's poem-titles, if analyzed, show certain recurring patterns that are interesting. They are never ironically self-reflexive. Two titles that belong to his juvenile period, namely "For Future Reference" and "Text," and one of his mature period, "PPS," hint at such a possibility. But a closer look suggests that Beckett means them literally rather than reflexively. Still, the title "Text" is significant because it implies that questioning of the definition of forms that eventually led to Beckett extending old forms or creating new ones. As a rule, Beckett titles his poems to make the form that he is using clear. Starting from "Gnome" that means epigram in Greek, and continuing with his enuegs, "Alba," sanies, serenas, "Cascando," threnes, "Envoi," "Song" and "Roundelay," this has been his dominant method of titling poems. The procedure has its uses and disadvantages. It makes the form known to the reader who would not have latched on to it otherwise. But the hint in the title that may eventually make the content of an obscure poem less opaque cannot usually be given in such titles. Beckett has titles that offer such hints too, but only occasionally. Titles like "Yoke of Liberty," "Calvary by Night" and "Da Tagte Es" are examples that match the poems by giving one an idea of the content of the poem beforehand that still remains valid as hint or clue even after one peruses it. Two other ways in which Beckett titles poems are by using proper or common nouns (e.g., "The Vulture," "Dortmunder," "Malacoda") and place-names (e.g., "Dieppe," "Saint-Lô"). Beckett has also resorted to the common technique of titling a poem by lifting a word or phrase from the text itself. Sometimes it is even the first word of the poem. The examples are "dread nay," "Something there," "thither" and "neither". Some of Beckett's fifty-odd English poems are named on the basis of who the narrator is and who the poem is written to or for. Thus, we find the titles "From the Only Poet to a Shining Whore," "Casket of Pralinen to a Daughter of a Dissipated Mandarin," "Hell Crane to Starling" and "To Nelly." When it came to collections of poetry, after his first collection called *Echo's Bones*, Beckett preferred names or titles that called attention to his form and hence they are usually titled just "Poèmes" or "Poems." One consistent feature of Beckett's interesting titles is that they are always allusive. This fact betrays that he was aware of the strategic part that titling plays in a poem as a device. Be it a title like "Whoroscope" which refers not only outwards to texts and people that are Beckettian and non-Beckettian but also downwards to the footnotes at the end of the poem, or one like "Saint-Lô" that conjures up a place, some of Beckett's biography and a historical situation, or even ones like "Cascando" and "neither" that refer either to Beckett's other texts or inwards to the core of the poem, this indirectly allusive nature makes the titles poetically charged verbal counters and intriguing components of the puzzles Beckett's poems mostly are. They are seldom uni-dimensional or to be taken for granted. In this context it must be stated that even Beckett's titles that refer to the form he employs are sometimes more complex than they seem. For example the title "Alba" refers not only to the aubade (dawn-song) but also to classical music and a fictional woman character of Beckett's. "The Vulture" is a title that, besides being symbolic and a literary allusion to a lyric by Goethe, acts also as the first words of the poem. This is an interesting variation on the possible uses a title can be put to. Even experiments with language (e.g., "Whoroscope"), titles that are foreign (e.g., "Da Tagte Es") and ones that question rules of grammar and punctuation (e.g., "Casket of Pralinen for a Daughter of a Dissipated Mandarin") are used. To wind up this section on Beckett's choice of titles for poems one can state that he viewed titling as an issue that contributes to improving the texture of the whole poem, if sensitively handled. Critics usually refer to Beckett's untitled poems by their first words or lines.

B. Punctuation

Beckett was an adept at English. As such he was no stranger to the rules of the language, including ones about punctuation marks. But, at first and indeed all throughout his artistic career as a writer, he was influenced not by linguistic purists like W.H. Hudson or Ford Maddox Ford but by the avant-garde writers like Joyce, Guillaume Apollinaire etc. Their influence shows up in major and even minor matters like punctuation. Thus initially Beckett can be seen making use of all the punctuation-marks available to the writer in English, but his usage is not according to the rule-book. Excess, misuse and abuse mark his handling of punctuation-marks. As a poetic device for the sake of differentiating between emphases that are subtle, we see him multiply capital letters, dots, hyphens, question-marks, exclamation-marks etc. The latter duo was his special weakness. In "Whoroscope," for example, the number of exclamation-marks amount to eighteen in a poem of ninety-nine lines. A veritable plethora of question-marks litters the landscape of the poem. Brackets, parentheses, commas, full-stops, colons, semi-colons and even words accented in the French manner (e.g., "belovèd" in 1.37) appear. All these are used sparingly in traditional poetry. Compounding with the help of the hyphen to form new words, like G.M. Hopkins's or Joyce's, was also a common feature of Beckett's early poems. Both the jettisoned poems and those of the years of wandering also experiment slightly with typography by using italics and occasionally putting titles, words or even entire lines in capitals. Examples of this can be seen in "Whoroscope" where the title is in capitals and in line ten the word "moving" appears the second time in italics for the sake of effect. All this, while excitingly contemporaneous, conveying the influences on Beckett and the impression of lively, colloquial speech, was not really Beckettian. Gradually, over the years, Beckett developed his own bare style of punctuating his writing. The mature poems make use of — and that too, sparingly — only capital letters, commas and full-stops apart from the small letters of the alphabet. Wherever possible, Beckett avoids even the former three tools of punctuation. He resembles, in this matter, a Gertrude Stein rather than appearance-oriented Concrete poets like Ian Hamilton Finlay. In a poem like "I would like my love to die," the absence of a title ensures that the only capital letter that appears is where Beckett follows the convention regarding the 'I.' No commas or full-stops interrupt the poem. In sticking to the convention of capitalizing the 'I' and the first letter of place names and proper nouns, Beckett shows that he is unlike e.e. cummings who holds the view that names, places and words like 'I' that describe the self need not necessarily be capitalized. Beckett started out by trying to use punctuation as an aid to enhance the poetic density of his works but soon seems to have come to the conclusion that omission is not a loss. He shows that much of the punctuation used in what is written is usually only an encrustation on the text placed there by tradition or habit and its absence would cause no difference to the meaning. Beckett punctuates his mature poems with the help of the line-break. The result is definitely a gain in poetic intensity. Beckett's mature manner of punctuation is not an effort to free the word from its 'signified' but rather to help it gain clarity. The result is, surprisingly enough, control of the word, the phrase and the line so that meanings multiply only where intended and seldom endlessly.

C. Lineation

In the twentieth century poetry is no longer connected to song because of the arrival of print. Both free verse and free prose are frequently written. One of the factors that helps a reader to differentiate between a piece of prose and one in verse in this context is lineation. Beckett retains this convention to separate his prose from his verse. But in *How It Is* and "Rockaby," — the former printed in stanzas and the latter in lines — he shows that this too is only a convention. In *Play* and "Come and Go," he demonstrates how prose arranged symmetrically, using laws of permutation and combination like the frogs' song in *Watt*, can sound just like verse. But these are the exceptions that help to prove the rule that lineation still matters. In his use of lineation too, Beckett shows a gradually changing viewpoint. His early poems experiment with lineation in a manner the equivalent of which can be seen in the *The Waste Land* and Pound's *Cantos*. Pound's experiments are more extreme because he makes use of the possibilities of spacing that typography provides, besides varying line-lengths. Beckett satisfies himself with the latter. But the length of his lines can vary to such an extent that one becomes aware that what is being offered is an ironic comment on the convention of lineation. In "Whoroscope," for example, there are lines that have in them only one or two words [e.g., "blood" (1.36), "An egg?" (1.2)], but also lines that often stretch to the next one. The longest line in the poem has in it fifteen words and that includes a compound word. The linereads: "Them were the days I sat in the hot-cupboard throwing Jesuits out of the skylight" (1.26).[1] As Beckett matured, this jaggedness of presenting lines of unequal length that are either too long or too short faded. Instead, his later poems usually contain lines that are not too short or long in comparison with the others in the poem. Although Beckett never returns to being totally traditional, in many respects one sees in him a reviving, partial interest in playing the game of literature from just outside or around its traditional conventions as one traces his journey from being a hot-headed modernist to an individualist in his art. This seems true whether the point being examined is his approach to titling, punctuation or lineation.

D. Rhyme and the Stanza

Prose has as its structure syntax, the sentence and the paragraph. In verse, the word or the phrase, the line and the stanza are the parallels. Since the revolution of modernism, these elements remain, but not as before. The ancients who hoped to master the art of verse worked within given classical frameworks, pouring their matter into forms, forcing their meanings into the requisite number of lines to make stanzas. Since the advent of poets like Rimbaud and techniques like 'surrealistic automatism' all this has changed. Modern poets prefer to let their organic genius dictate where stanzas should end and how many lines should be found in each. Rhyme, a necessary adjunct to the stanza, was abandoned or used more subtly. In his early phase Beckett made use of traditional rhymes and stanzaic forms only in "Gnome" and his sonnets. All the other poems show a conspicuous absence of rhyme, except at a subliminal level, and the presence of stanzas that can range from having one line to ten or eleven. The convenience of the poet decides all this. But in Beckett's mature phase, bits of which can be glimpsed in his early poems like "The Vulture" and "Da Tagte Es," while rhyme and metre remain as points to be decided arbitrarily, the couplet and the quatrain gradually swim into view as having a grip on Beckett. The balladic quatrain keeps erupting into brief poems in the hands of Beckett. "Gnome," "Da Tagte Es," "Dieppe," "I would like my love to die" and "Saint-Lô" have four lines each and the rhythm is definitely that of the quatrain, albeit rough. The poems "Echo's Bones" and "they come," although having five lines each, are like extended quatrains. In the sonnet in *Dream* and in "Roundelay" Beckett makes masterly use of the flexibility of the quatrain. These examples perhaps hint at the fact that English is a language that gives itself more easily to couplets and quatrains than to stanzaic patterns like the terza rima. In choosing the length of his stanzas or poems, brevity seems to be Beckett's watchword. While the length is mostly arbitrary, no poem of Beckett can actually be called long. Some aspire to the title, but none have the concerted appeal to length of an "Eve of St.Agnes" or a "Rime of the Ancient Mariner." The short poem is Beckett's specialty. It can be seen that in such matters as rhyme, the stanza and the size of poems, Beckett eventually developed his own natural rules that resemble traditional ones, although he did not adhere to those of the past. There is, consequently, a balance between tightness and freedom in his poems that look like some of the better poems of the surrealists in matters of prosody as a result.

E. Metre and Rhythm

Speech, prose and verse have different rhythms. When the rhythm of verse is made symmetrical, metre comes into being. Metre, a very controversial area as far as accurate analysis is concerned, was one of the key components of verse till poets like Whitman and Pound declared war on it. The European influence also led to the demolition of the idea that metre is a cardinal virtue. Beckett showed himself capable of writing in metre in his sonnets, "Gnome," "To Nelly" etc. But what is remarkable about the majority of his poems is the absence of regular metrical arrangements. His early poems have the strong rhythmic patterns of speech and are poetic without being metrical. This does not preclude a metrical analysis of them. His mature poems show a greater tendency to metre. The rhythm becomes graphically that of poetry and slowly, in poems like "Roundelay" and "Thither," purely musical. The result is definitely soothing to the ear. What is written sounds clearly like verse but even here Beckett is not writing with any particular metre in mind. It is with a certain beat and rhythm that he writes his more musical pieces, like a musician who prefers notes and melodies to chord-structure and progressions. Metrical analysis of Beckett's poems will show, however, a surprising amount of diversity and richness because he has, over the years, made use of all the standard 'feet' like the iamb, the anapest, the trochee, the dactyl, the spondee and the pyrrhic. He has also used metrical lines that vary in the number of feet contained in them from the monometer to the heptameter. But it may be wiser to state that Beckett's early poems are written more in quantitative metre than in the metre of quality that is based on stress and accent. The features highlighted in his prosaic poems are not stress or accent but alliteration, consonance, assonance, images and onomatopoeia. Euphony begins to play its rightful share in the mature poems like "Roundelay." In short, much of Beckett's verse belongs to that category called free verse and some of it definitely slips over into being free prose. In "Whoroscope," the notes of the poem are in prose proper. This creates an interesting hybrid that cannot be properly classified in terms of any rhythmic or metrical form. In the last play Beckett wrote, "What Where" (1983), he again mixes verse that is musical and verges on being metrical with the prose-sections creating an even more complex hybrid that can be called drama that aspires towards conditions of dance, music and poetry at the same time. As a youth Beckett abandoned metre but in his maturity he allows its ghost to haunt his verse and even his prose, as Marjorie Perloff has pointed out in her excellent study of Beckett's novella "Ill Seen Ill Said."[2] The result is an enhancement in the cadenced feel of what he writes that makes it a feast for the auditory imagination. As was stated before in the course of this study, Beckett has been able to reproduce onomatopoeically, in his verse, the rhythms of walking and cycling with the help of alliteration and 'cacophony.' The different types of walking, that is, the slow, the fast, the restless etc., have been explored by him continuously and effectively in his verse. He has consistently striven to reproduce its rhythms in the sounds, images and meanings of the words he chooses in poems starting from the enuegs in *Echo's Bones* to "Roundelay" and "neither." Beckett's views on diction and prosody and his practice fit in more with the desire to carve well two inches of ivory than any ambition of writing metre that others would not willingly let die. In this sense and in his tireless experimentation in prosodic matters Beckett shows a resemblance to the Metaphysical poets like John Donne, in spirit.

F. The Image

Poetry has been image-oriented from time immemorial. In Beckett's hands, the concept of the image became refined. He knew clearly that "it is naturally in the image that . . . profound and abstruse self-consciousness first emerges with the least loss of integrity."[3] In his early phase, his poems are littered with surrealistic images, the connections between which are often indecipherable. In this he was only following the best of the many poets of his age who belonged to various avant-garde movements like Expressionism (German), Symbolism, Surrealism, the Aesthetic Decadence, Dadaism (French), Imagism and Vorticism (British and American). Poets as diverse as Arthur Rimbaud, Charles Baudelaire, André Breton, T.E. Hulme and Ezra Pound were all experimenting with the concreteness and sensuousness of images, not to mention their ability to act as symbols, fantasies, opaque objects, creations, figures of speech etc. A common link was disjointedness, i.e., the connection between images remaining potential and to be activated by the reader rather than hidden and available only to an elite. Beckett manages to rival poets like Dylan Thomas with memorable images that can be abstract or concrete, like "the tempest of emblems" ("Alba," 1. 13) and "knees of stone" ("Serena II," 1.52). "Cascando" has in it many individual images that are brilliant.

> the grapples clawing blindly the bed of want
> bringing up the bones the old loves
> sockets filled once with eyes like yours
> ....
> the black want splashing their faces (1. 6-9, 11)
>
> the churn of stale words in the heart again
> love love love thud of the old plunger
> pestling the unalterable
> whey of words (1. 25-28)

The above images are primarily visual and auditory, but with a stretch of the imagination it can be seen how they also incite the tactile, olfactory, gustatory and kinaesthetic senses.

Beckett is often seen to coin a neologism to conjure up an image that is semi-abstract but haunting. "Worsdshed" ("Cascando") is an example that comes instantly to mind. "Whoroscope" is another. In his use of images in his early poems, Beckett was fully aware of the power of imagery to be figurative and discreetly symbolic. As a result, by indirectly working as metaphors and metonyms without fixed referents, his imagery always opens his poems out into being signifiers with vast connotations. The ambiguity inherent in the absence of precise clues or connections that he fails to provide helps this process.

In his mature poems we see Beckett's view of the image and imagery being refined and made exacting, perhaps under the influence of film-techniques. He substitutes freewheeling through many images for a startling procedure. His poems concentrate exclusively on a single image that is then sharpened or allowed to melt away with the help of variations on the same. This highlighting of a single 'frame' or 'shot' manages to hint at a story and is surprisingly dramatic. Here what comes into play is not the experimental possibilities of the word but its ability to be almost transparent so that the reader is vouchsafed an experience of an aesthetic world that is almost real. Repeatedly, in poems like "Dieppe," "Something there," "Roundelay," "thither" and "neither," this approach is taken. This is surely an area in which Beckett can be called original. He melds euphony, an image and its variations, incompleteness and obscurity into poems that reverberate with sparse richness as a result. They almost achieve the ineffable, becoming something more than just words. It is as if the words are becoming objectified. Even in a poem as early as the "The Vulture" Beckett's tendency towards such distillation is visible, but eventually he learnt to write consistently in this mode. Perhaps concentrating on a single image is not a new idea in the world of poetry, since poems like Wordsworth's "The Solitary

Reaper" also make use of it. But to do it in a photographic and cinematic way and create an effect that is dramatic and hints at narrative, crossing the different literary genres with that of choreography and music, all within the "closed space" of a lyric or short poem is something unheard of. Yet, in "Roundelay" and "thither" Beckett does all this, carrying imagery to new heights. Here he is truly original.

G. Allusiveness

While allusiveness is not a specifically poetic device, it is used so rampantly in Beckett's poems that it deserves separate consideration. In Beckett's early poems allusions literally riddle the text. They constantly point outwards to other texts by other authors, to Beckett's earlier texts, to people who are living or dead, to things and places that are imaginary or real and to acts, situations and events that may be mythical, historical, literary, biographical or even anachronisms. Examples of all these types of allusions can be found in "Whoroscope" and the longer poems in *Echo's Bones*. The pun, which is also a kind of semantic allusion, abounds in Beckett's early texts. But in the mature poems both external allusions and puns disappear almost totally. Instead, internal allusions, controlled punning and intertextual echoes that are strictly Beckettian dominate. Explicit allusiveness is exchanged for implicitness. The result: poems that, because of repetitions and connections between phrases that point backwards, read like 'palimpsests' of all of Beckett's works. Centrifugally, the poems reveal a Beckettian ideolect that suggests clearly the ambience of Beckett's irreplaceable personality. A poem like "Roundelay," for instance, for one familiar with Beckett's entire canon, becomes nearly inexhaustible. It refers to all his works that make use of the metaphors of walking, the sea and the strand as symbolic substitutes for the processes of living, death and dying. The list would include poems in *Echo's Bones*, "Dieppe," other poems, *Molloy*, "Footfalls," *Embers*, "Company" etc. In inverting the technique of allusiveness towards implicitness, Beckett has thus produced interesting effects and original results, especially this feel of the text as a palimpsest.

H. Language

In the early poems of Beckett, language appears as an entity that is not only polysemous but spilling over in every sense into different kinds of excess. The influence of Joyce can be strongly sensed. A clutter of puns, multilingual ism, compound words, neologisms, the unnatural usage of words forced into new syntactical relationships etc., are common. The result is complicated rather than complex. To all this is added the traditional pot-pourri of poetic license, like the use of archaism, inversion, grammatical misnomers etc. The result is often cacophonic and although intended is neither true to Beckett's potential nor something special in comparison with the same experiments carried out by his contemporaries and equals. But Beckettsoon found his metier and view of language and there sult was, in both prose and verse, excellent. The puns were sloughed off, except where essential. Neologisms became rare. Compound words vanished. Gradually Beckett developed a language that deconstructed syntax but abstained from all manner of linguistic excess. The result was a set of words and phrases that adhered together in spite of being fragments and helped verse to transcend into the domain of poetry. In piece after piece this (un-) scrupulous attitude to language of one who knew his grammar emerges and as a result both the flaws of English and its deep structures and strengths are exposed to readers, sometimes afresh. Reading Beckett's poems "I would like my love to die," for example, one becomes aware that the lack of gender-specific pronouns in English can be a weakness or an asset, depending on the context. Such insights and details come to the surface when language is being probed by a writer who is sensitive to his medium, without his having to state his interesting mistakes and findings the way a linguist would. Beckett applies his insights in his poems and leaves it to his reader to deduce them and gain a richer understanding of the nature of the language he is reading. In moving away from the beaten Joycean and grammarian tracks Beckett has won for English, in texts like *Worstward Ho*, (1989) beautiful and extensive poetic possibilities that have swum fully into our sight only now.

In short, to write an epitaph on this section on poetic devices and Beckett's views and practice of them, it can be said that in most of these matters Beckett is selective, contemporary and not special. But in his use of imagery and allusiveness, as well as his ability to carve out a style of his own and a new kind of poetry, he is without peer. In the better poems of his maturity these factors can be clearly seen.

Aesthetic Forms and Structures

A point that keeps coming up for discussion in connection with Beckett's poems is the fact that they are few in number. This seems a negative sign to many. But the richness of his slender poetic output has to be read to be believed. As a result, any analysis of his poems will reveal no lack of material to be dealt with. His brevity inevitably calls forth verbal plenitude on the part of the critics. This is something that has been noted in respect to his prose and novels and plays. It is true of his poems too. Thus, for example, after having studied very briefly the poetic techniques that Beckett employs, when one turns one's attention to the poetic forms be experimented with and the hidden structures of his poems one finds such a wealth of versatility that it is startling.

From fifty-odd poems, nearly as many forms, modifications, extensions, transformations, subversions and structures can be elicited. Most of them are clearly implied or implicated by the author himself. This is what is staggering to a reader who unwittingly stumbles on the few poems in English of Beckett, expecting the task of appreciation to be easy.

Beckett's first poem, "For Future Reference," sets the trend, showing us his avidness to test the old forms and explore new avenues. The poem is written in the form of a direct interior monologue. The influence of Browning is evident. The structure is that of the oneiric narrative. This is experimental. From there it is only a short step to "Whoroscope," where the form is extended to be a direct 'dramatic' interior monologue. The structure becomes that of the psychological narrative. The footnotes in prose make the poem a hybrid form like *The Waste Land*, one that can be called for want of a better name 'the annotated poem.' Annotated poems are now common but at the time of the appearance of "Whoroscope," although Eliot's poem had been the forerunner, Beckett's attempt was not only an imitation but a daring one. In the poems, "Text" and "Casket of Pralinen . . .," Beckett experimented with narratives that adopted the stream-of-consciousness technique to verse and made use of multiple points of view and voices to establish a structure of balance and tension. In all these four poems, 'the associative paradigm' and free verse work as elements that unify the disparate pulls within them.

The eulogy in verse or the ironic tribute was a form that appealed to Beckett. Four of his poems belong to this category. "Whoroscope" pays reverence to René DesCartes, "From the Only Poet . . . " to Dante, "Return to the Vestry" to Pierre de Ronsard and "Home Olga" is a homage to Beckett's then living mentor James Joyce. These four poems are not blind encomiums.

Beckett has written sonnets. He has also experimented with the lyric, writing love lyrics like "Yoke of Liberty." "From the Only Poet . . . " can be considered as not only a eulogy but also as a love poem. The sonnet "At last I find in my confusèd soul" is, similarly, a love song. But it also conceals, as does "Calvary by Night," the elements from which 'parody' is obtained. Both "Whoroscope" and "Calvary by Night" are examples of Beckett's attempt to create linear, circular and spiral patterns simultaneously in his work. Hence, appropriately, the poem "Whoroscope" begins and ends with the word "hour," but meanwhile temporal loops and the chronological beginning, middle and end of DesCartes' life are also narrated. In "Calvary by Night" the same effect is created, perhaps more effectively, by the fact that the words that begin the poem end it in inverse order while the cyclical budding, blooming and wilting of a flower is described. The latter is a symbol for the structure of birth, life and death. Even typographically, this design is incorporated visually into the poem by the length of the lines being first brief, then lengthy, then brief again.

"Return to the Vestry," besides being a tribute is also elegiac. "Home Olga" is an acrostic. "Hell Crane to Starling" is an immature carpe diem. The longer poems like "Text" and "Casket of Pralinen . . . " make the point that poems can be prosaic, not dramatic and 'indirect' while still being Browingesque, Joycean and modern in the manner of Eliot, Pound and the European avant-garde poets. All these are safe inferences to make. The poem that perhaps points to the most number of forms is "Gnome." It refers to the German xenien, as mentioned earlier, the English equivalents of which are the aphorism, the maxim, the proverb the epigram, and the riddle. The gnome itself is a Grecian form akin to the Hebrew proverb that makes use of parallelism. The forms and structures so far mentioned are the ones Beckett tried out, experimented on, extended, altered, modified and revived, with slight touches of subversion, in his jettisoned poems. Even where he does not subvert much, as is the case in his handling of sources like Dante and Ronsard, he still makes the difference between his mentors' views and his clear.

In the years of wandering Beckett continued with his restless shape-changing habit as far as forms and structures are concerned. His Echo's Bones contains, apart from the prologue "The Vulture" and the proverbial riddle "Da Tagte Es" that is also a communal elegy or lament, adaptations of 'old' forms like the enueg, the elegy proper ("Malacoda"), the serenade, the aubade and the epilogue. Inevitably, this also ensures that the connected forms of the planh (the Provençal lament) and the nocturne are also in the picture. In Echo's Bones Beckett invents the form of the sanie. Its structure is that of an objective correlative to gaseous and liquid states of being. It mimes physical discharges, basically. Other traditional structures one recognizes easily in the collection are those of fiction, autobiography, the journey and the voyage. Elements of the tragicomic, the bawdy and the mock-heroic are also present in the structures of these poems, not to mention the picaresque. "Malacoda" is not only an elegy but also an occasional poem. "Enueg II" is of the same ilk. Both were occasioned by the deaths of Beckett's loved ones. "Saint-Lô" is another of Beckett's occasional poems. In *Echo's Bones*, Beckett makes the discovery that the list is a fitting structure for a poem. This is in "Enueg I." As a result, repeatedly, in poems like "Ooftish," the list becomes the structure for the poem. Like "Da Tagte Es," many of Beckett's poems function as riddles. "Dieppe," "Saint-Lô" and "We shall be here all night" fit this pattern.

Since 1935 Beckett became an adept at juggling with forms and structures as far as his poems are concerned. "Cascando," another new form that he borrowed, this time from another aesthetic medium, that of music, is also a carpe diem and a lyrical love poem. It has a tripartite structure like "Malacoda," a structure that is shared by key Beckettian texts like "Come and Go" and *How It Is*. After the sanie, 'the cascando' is Beckett's second contribution to poetic form. It is an entropic form, suggesting a dying away and hence can be reproduced in any genre as Beckett proved when he later wrote another "Cascando" that is a radio-play. The tripartite structure of "Malacoda" and "Cascando" may be considered Aristotelian, Dantescan or that of a sonata. If considered as the latter, "Cascando" comes complete with a prelude, overture, major and minor chords and themes, a leitmotif, melody, harmony, point and counterpoint and a postlude.

"Ooftish," the list-poem, is Promethean and an enueg. It is in "they come" that Beckett again breaks fresh ground. The form is declarative. But it is nameless. At most, it can be called a short poem. The lyrical note is absent. In the context of the collection ("Poèmes 1937-'39") the poem works as a fitting prelude. It is the structure of "they come" that is of much importance. For the first time Beckett introduces a grid of structure to support his work horizontally and vertically. Repetition and variation and permutation and combination are the two arms of this grid. Using this potent combination Beckett wrote five of the poems — "We shall be here all night", the two threnes, the song of the frogs and "Watt will not" — in *Watt*. By the time one reads "Watt will not" one realizes that he mastered it. The other four do not show the same finish since content and form do not become satisfactorily one in them.

All the attempts at poetry in Watt remain interesting for various reasons. The first poem in the novel "To Nelly," seems to be a parody of the archaic 'epithalamion' in its parts. The small absurd poem Arsene sings and the two threnes (threnodies) Watt hears in his head because he is prone to schizophrenia suggest that Beckett was moving out of the idea that verse should subvert itself by adopting the structure of prose into a realization that music is an essential adjunct to poetry. As usual, he presents this in the typical Beckettian manner of deep-rooted irreverence. In the song of the frogs by making use of only three sounds (krik, krak and krek) without meaning, repeating and combining them with mathematical exactness, Beckett creates an astonishing tour de force that hints at the strength of music, minimalism and verse while at the same time invalidating the seriousness of these enterprises as they amount only to, metaphysically speaking, ineffective "croaks." Consequently perhaps, a character in his radio-play "Words and Music" is named Croak and his sequence "PPS" was described by him as 'croaks.' Since Watt, however, perhaps as a result of these experiments, both "the song" and the musical element, not to mention his repetitive and permutative tendencies have become forms or structures readily available to him and he has used them again and again. The two poems in "Words and Music" are songs. "Roundelay" and "thither" repeat, vary, permute and combine to near perfection. The ancient forms of the incantation and the chant are invoked by Beckett here, but in the modern context. Beckett's "neither" was performed as a song besides being published as a poem.

The last poem in *Watt* which later appeared as the "Envoi / Tailpiece" to Beckett's *Collected Poems 1930-'78* makes possible a form that is purely 'interrogative' since the entire text is a set of questions. The list is once more the structure of this significant little poem.

In his short story or novella "First Love" Beckett has written an epitaph. Snippets of verse that appear in Beckett's prose works need to be studied as separate poems because they usually do not lose any of their intrinsic form, structure or meaning when divorced from their original context. The poem "Watt will not" is an exception to this rule, along with the two insignificant quatrains in *Malone Dies* that are mock love-poems and said to be written by Malone's character MacMann to Moll while he is being treated by her in the lunatic asylum in that remarkable novel.

The poems "my way is in the sand flowing" and "I would like my love to die" belong to the 'declarative' category. The form is lyrical, but the lyric is extended into being flexible enough to accommodate any emotion. The structure of these poems is actually dramatic; that of the 'soliloquy' or 'aside' refined into being meditative verse that is capable of cadence and nuance and rivetingly complex. But "I would like my love to die" is not as effective as "my way is in the sand flowing" because of a certain flaw Beckett makes in his use of the language. The use of the soliloquy here is the natural evolution of Beckett's earlier external or interior 'monologues' and its apt end. In the poems "Watt will not" and "what would I do without this world faceless incurious" we see Beckett introduce another structure, that of the Socratic dialogue. But his dialogues are not stripped of sophistry. The form is like that of the 'catechism,' where a question is asked and an answer is given. Since Beckett is post-modern, although the exchange seems significant neither the question nor the answer is anything but oblique.

As was stated earlier, elements of 'metaverse' rear up occasionally in a few of Beckett's poems like "Casket of Pralinen . . . " and "Sanies I." But it is a thread or form that does not grow stronger in his poems. However, in his plays and novels meta-theatrical and meta-fictional tendencies keep growing into a major form and structure. "Catastrophe" and *The Unnamable* are the examples and results.

While it is clear that Beckett has extended the lyric's capability, he does not move entirely out of the egocentric Cartesian framework on which the lyric leans for its survival. The ego still continues to exist, even if only as an impersonal recorder or scribe. Beckett tries to counter a simplistic definition of the self not by showing voices in multiplicity like Pound or as he himself did in "Text" but by the structure of selection and omission. By selecting indeterminate words like the pronouns to play a key part in his poems, or by omitting limiting clues in them he makes the lyric an open-ended form whereby multiplicity is made possible. For example, in the poem "thither" the phrase "for one/so little" is so clear and yet so ambiguous that its referent or signified wilily refuses to be fixed. This open-endedness and indefiniteness has made it possible for Beckett to incorporate into his works structures that suggest 'entropy' and 'eternal recurrence' as well as 'gyres' ably. In fact, poems like "Roundelay," "thither" and "neither" have a core of precisely such far-reaching metaphysical structures and implications. "Roundelay" is significant also for the fact that it is a borrowal, adaptation and transformation of an archaic form. To the names of the gnome and enueg can be added that of the roundelay as one of the forms that Beckett has tried to rejuvenate. His esotericism and his ability to choose forms no one else will try to revive or attempt after him is also noteworthy in this context.

Beckett's forms open out not only on to other structures and genres in literature but also to the other plastic arts. No one can read "The Vulture" without realizing that painting is the art that has been a major influence on it. The movement of the figures in some of Beckett's poems like "Roundelay" and "thither" is stylized and has the beauty of dance-choreography. Music is evoked everywhere, especially in the later poems. The influence of the freefall of jazz appears in Beckett's juvenile poems. That of classical music penetrates his aubades and serenades. In his mature poems, it is the spirit of modern composers like Philip Glass that one feels; not as an influence but as an affinity. Film, theatre and photography have also left their imprint on these poems. This can be seen by the fact that the mature poems give one the impression that they could easily be translated into these media while retaining the same intensity. Beckett was clearly aware of the differences and the sameness of all these art-forms.

All the poems we have looked at so far in terms of aesthetic forms and structures have recognizable forms or subversions. But in the two strange poems Beckett wrote in the seventies, outwardly, form and structure are absent. They are "dread nay" and "Something there." They are remarkable for this reason. But a closer look reveals that while form is absent, they do have unique structures that can be pinpointed. Both use incomplete predication, i.e., a structure of omission and mystification, to bewilder the reader. "Undecidability"[4] prevails. The classic archetype of all structures, whether semantic or aesthetic, is the Hegelian dialectic. Here, a term is introduced (the thesis) and a counter-term (the anti-thesis) arises. The result is aesthetic or semantic conflict. Depending on whether the conflict is resolved or not, a 'synthesis' may occur. In the two poems mentioned above, the reader brings to the poems his need for clarity as the thesis. The poems play along with this need for a while and then suddenly refuse to, creating the anti-thesis which is the absence of meaning. Later, even when it returns to clarity, the thread has been lost and the reader cannot induce a neat synthesis from the semiotic fragments the texts present. In spite of all, communication occurs at a non-verbal level due to the atmosphere the words of the poems create. Imagination triumphs over the intellect and the reader is given a brief taste of fantasy, horror, fiction and "Nietzschean insecurity,"[5] where he enters the gulf between meaning and its absence. These two poems draw their strength from their potency rather than from their finish.

In his collections, Beckett constantly drew on the sequence as the structure that inspired him. His last sequence, "PPS," shows the adaptation of another form, this time from the world of letter-writing. It widens his range. As he said once, where forms are concerned he actually did experiment with some "two or three hundred"[6] and in his poems one sees where many of these came from.

To close this section on the aesthetic forms and structures of Beckett's poems in English, it must be stated that Beckett reveals a thorough knowledge of the conventions of the discourses of poetry, literature and art that shows that he was no dilettante. He blazes a new trail, but it is with the awareness of both his weaknesses and strengths and it is this that makes his ability to enlarge the frame of what is poetically possible convincing.

A few words about the forms and structures Beckett did not attempt may also be illuminating. The epic in verse, the long poem, poems based on actions and events, society verse and the ode are forms he never tried out. This is revealing of his passive and pessimistic personality. He was one to whom 'heroic' poems would hardly suggest themselves. It is also an insight into the crisis-ridden spirit and state of literature at present. The spirits of the epic and the satire have fled from the domain of verse to the realms of prose. Homer and Swift have given way to J.R.R. Tolkien and Beckett, both of whom excelled in prose and refused to devote much time to poems. Still, what little they have left behind in verse shows in miniature the same excellence as their prose and so most of it is worth preserving.

The Major Theme

In the preceding chapters of this study, the fact that Beckett's themes are innumerable has been adequately hinted at. The semantic underpinning of his work is primarily aesthetic, metaphysical and psychological. But temporal and spatial disciplines like history and geography also play their part in it. Traces of theology and mythology appear rarely. While Beckett is indisputably a form-oriented writer, one cannot ascertain in the face of his work over the years that he gave to the aspects of content and meaningless importance. His attempt was to do what he thought Joyce and Proust had done,[7] to unify form and content so perfectly that no one could separate the lantern from the light. This emerges from his oeuvre. But in his interviews and critical pieces he admitted his failure to establish the equilibrium once for all.

In his poems one sees that where content is concerned the structures Beckett employed are more often psychological or philosophical than aesthetic. The influence of thinkers like DesCartes, Kant, Hegel and Heidegger can be sensed. The presence of Freud can also be felt. But occasionally Beckett converts form itself into the central content of a poem and the structures of poetics and aesthetics predominate then. In the light of post-modern critical theories, Beckett's poems can also be seen as typical examples of the technique of 'deferral' whereby meaning can be potential, dissolved, delayed partially, endlessly multiplied, absent, symbolized or even parodied as non-existent.

Critics have stated, as the present author has reiterated, that Beckett's leading themes include the key ones explored in most of the important works of not only this age but most ages. Loneliness, solitude, the dislike of learning, the love of wandering, the conflicts between the subject and the object (the other) and the self and the world (society, family, teachers, etc.), the preference of emotion over intellect, experience over knowledge, freedom over bondage, fears that are sexual and otherwise, the desire for wish-fulfilment and pleasure that gives precedence to dreams, wordplay and the unconscious, youth, revolt, rebellion, ambition of the Promethean and Satanic variety rooted in pride that resultantly mocks God, suffering, love for literature, art and humanity-as opposed to the disciplines of the intellect like science-can all be glimpsed as themes in his first poem "For Future Reference" retrospectively. The rest of the jettisoned poems buttress these initial probings by adding themes that are new in Beckett's writings but ancient in literature like birth, living, dying, death, life, religion, locale, nation, language, style, form, individuality, Christ, universality, temporality and eternity, the spatial and the infinite, sex in its variations and perversions, complexes like the oedipal, aesthetic influences and affinities, social concerns, the importance of the family, the urban atmosphere, the presence of Nature, the burden of History, theology, myths etc. Principles of selection, compression, suggestivity and metonymy have enabled Beckett's immature and effective poems to be packed with themes galore. In *Echo's Bones* the influx of themes continues. Exile, separation, metamorphoses, loss, sorrow, tragedy, the implacable nature of destiny and the existentialist on nihilistic attitude of bitter resignation to a life that the author attempts to eviscerate and control by gaining mastery over his art where he can make his secrets about himself and his painful knowledge of life bearable are a few of the important ones. The usual themes like Time and Memory are also included.

After 1935, the pace at which the new themes proliferated became less frantic. This was because Beckett's style became ascetic. He changed from imitating the encyclopedic clutter of the Joycean style that assumes that tomes of information are interesting if unknown. It also happened because Beckett was gaining in maturity. The shift was away from the horizontal dimensions of meaning which are often connected with the cultural, socioeconomic and political aspects of the milieu the writer is entrenched into the vertical dimensions where the psyche, ontology, aesthetics etc., matter more. Beckett was not really drawn to ethical or epistemological inquiry. It is the imaginative psychic mode of existence and his "ontological anxiety"[8] that is foregrounded in his later poems repeatedly. These themes are significant undercurrents in his early poems. In the poems of the mature phase they become leading.

To examine the main thread of Beckett's poems that is also related to the title of this book, for the first time as yet but in depth, one must turn first to the definitions of the words Nothingness and Being. The Webster's dictionary's brief definitions are suitable. Being is defined as: "1. (a) the quality or state of having existence. (b) (i) something conceivable as existing, (ii) something that actually exists, (iii) the totality of existing things, (c) conscious existence: LIFE. 2. the qualities that constitute an existent thing: ESSENCE, etc."[9] Nothingness is roughly defined as: "the quality or state of (a) NON-EXISTENCE, (b) utter insignificance (c) DEATH. . . VOID, EMPTINESS. A metaphysical entity opposed to and devoid of Being and regarded by some existentialists as the ground of anxiety."[10] One of the ways of developing a constant approach to all of Beckett's works like his poems is to consider them as attempts via expression to move from the ground of Nothingness to the state of Being. In his juvenile poems Beckett does not seem conscious that this is perhaps his major emphasis. But gradually both textually and in his own statements about his art this subject begins to present itself as central. Beckett outlines his trajectory but makes use of the

Heideggerian premise that Being and Nothingness are finally the same as if it is his own. The promise itself is a logical and epistemological faux-pas, although rhetorically it may hold.

The artist cannot represent Nothingness or Being. He can only offer metaphors for them in his medium. As a matter of fact, as far as Art is concerned, such abstract metaphysical concepts inhere only in their metaphors and can be projected only through them, tangentially. The artist can only 'try' to express, through his outpourings, Nothingness and the journey where transmutation, transformation or transposition takes place so that Being may come into existence. In a sense his attempt is foredoomed to failure since neither Nothingness nor Being can be expressed. His art can be successfully expressive only of transition, metamorphosis and change. It is, in short, a suitable metaphor for the state of 'becoming' which is a process, but as far as reaching its goal or revealing its origin goes it is evidently non-expressive. This tense dilemma is the one Beckett encounters and explores unflinchingly in successive stages in his poems and other major works.

All this philosophizing can be explained with brief examples that are chronologically arranged from the poems so that the practical aspects and application of this line of thinking can be made clear. The background of the argument is initially Cartesian dualism and Hegelian dialecticism. To start with it may help to turn back to Beckett's first poem "For Future Reference." It was initially titled "Reality and Beyond," a presumptuous title because Beckett was not yet ready to take on a theme of such vast metaphysical implications. But in that title the seed and germ of what is being discussed is contained. "Beyond" is a metaphor for essence/Essence and being/Being, while "Reality" stands for the real/existence and becoming. The movement is, for Beckett, away from the latter pair to the former. In the poem we see its surface bristling with dualistic antagonisms, tensions and conflict. A whole series of metaphors of and for Reality clash with its counterparts that bespeak the Beyond. The result is hopelessly irresolute. Neither "Reality" nor the "Beyond" are defined and reality is not transcended, but the modus operandi is already set. It remained but for Beckett to find the exact metaphors whereby this content-centred and structure-oriented dialectic could be made manifest to its best aesthetic advantage. In "Whoroscope" the dialectic works, not overtly but as a significant undercurrent. Its presence is marked by the introduction of the egg as a symbol. What does it signify? It is as if the whole thing is stage-managed or tailor-made. What better symbol could there be for Nothingness, becoming and Being than an egg? It is 'nothing' as yet, yet in it 'being' is coming into existence. DesCartes' life, everyman's life, is also similarly potent, pregnant with possibility and metaphoric in miniature. In the course of the poem the fragile balance or illusion of beauty is exchanged, exposed or destroyed for reality. The egg is destined to become an omelette. The chicken's life is aborted. The whiteness of the eggshell is shown to be deceptively soothing. Nothing comes from 'nothing' and 'being' remains unattainable. DesCartes' life, Beckett hints, although he was an incisive philosopher and mathematician, is similarly not exempt from the *hamartia* (tragic flaw) engineered by destiny that ensures that the quest of man to become more than nothing is doomed to failure. Beckett's view of man is akin to that of Pascal's in the first half of the Pensèes. But unlike Pascal Beckett does not think of redemption as possible. As "Whoroscope" suggests in miniscule, all that is possible is to keep emerging from nothing in the attempt to reach a "second/starless inscrutable hour."[11] The view is akin to that of the great tragic dramatists of Greece.

Thus, throughout the rest of Beckett's poems "non-expression" weaves in and out as an inadequate metaphor for Being and Nothingness and an adequate one for the process or flux of 'becomingness' or 'decay.' Meanwhile, the metaphors for these four verbal counters are kept changing. Beckett does this adroitly. The result is excitingly kaleidoscopic. Metaphors pile up on metaphors and breed suggestive images that defy explication because the sign divorced of referents and meanings raises multiple possibilities. Through a non-expressive art Beckett tries to overcome the roots of resistance in language and solitary moments of transcendence swim across our eyes in his poetry with increasing regularity and grandeur, like shooting stars bridling his anguish at his failure, according to the present reader.

To return to tracing out the appearance of the pair Nothingness and Being in the rest of Beckett's jettisoned poems, in artful guises that seem strange, a brief list may help.

The Poem	Nothingness	Becoming/ Decaying	Being
From the Only Poet to a Shining Whore	Inferno	Purgatorio	Paradiso
Casket of Pralinen to a Daughter of a Dissipated Mandarin	Beauty	Critical self-reflexivity (aesthetic)	Truth
Text	Art	Appearance	Reality
Yoke of Liberty	The Femme Fatale	Awareness of the other as pitiable/The power of temptation.	The Self
Hell Crane to Starling	Impotence	Desire	Virility
Return to the Vestry	Eros	Thanatos	Anteros

Home Olga	Imitation	Discipleship	Originality
Gnome	Die Lehrjahre (squandering)	Die Wanderjahre (wanderlust)	"Courage"
Sonnet	Sexual desire	Sexual intercourse	An aesthetic experience of quasi-mystic transcendence as an aftermath
Calvary by Night	The womb	Fertilization	Creation

No rough chart can pay full justice to the multi-facetedness of the antagonisms that Beckett generates with words. His texts hold more binary opposites and trinities than this simplification depicts. But an extensive list would be confusing, besides being untrue to the fact that it is the dyadic and triadic structure involved that is more important than the actual different metaphors for Nothingness, becoming, decay and Being that stay out of or carve themselves into play in each text.

In *Echo's Bones* the poems continue to reflect the same design. The pattern becomes clearer. In "The Vulture," the bird is an agent that wishes to bring about authentic creation from the 'chaos' within the head. But the quest is portrayed with the end not in sight. The title of the collection is an image that houses Being, with reference to a myth. Echo has actually been transformed into stone. But within the poems themselves it is the metamorphoses that are taking place that are delineated, not the outcome. Emblems that indicate that this change is taking place recur. In "Alba" and "Dortmunder" the woman becomes an instrument whereby the experiencing self can enter, through the door of coitus and with the help of music, a place that is a temporary release or 'being' with a small b. In the sonnet "At last I find in my confusèd soul" this counterfeit of Being was already suggested. Like the vulture in the first poem of the collection, the woman is the seeming harbinger or catalyst of Being in these two poems. But what is offered and experienced is only a similitude of the real thing and both the poems end on notes of dissolution where the conceived moment oozes away into 'emptiness,' the individualized form of Nothingness. The restless enuegs, sanies and serenas are filled with the strain of living and gradually 'becomingness' is revealed as a coin that has two sides. Its positive side is its expectancy that Being can be brought forth. Its negative side is the strain of the journey or the voyage, apt poetic metaphors for which are the verbs that dominate the collection such as flying, walking, cycling, lying, sailing etc., that reminds us that just as living is also dying and becoming ends in decay, creating can also be destroying. In "Malacoda" the mention of butterflies and "the imago" suggests the cycle of chrysalis. But the final "nay" of the poem denies Being hope of birth. As the collection begins to take on a life of its own, a shift in Beckett's perception also becomes evident. Death gradually assumes an absolute position. It stands for both Being and Nothingness according to philosophers like Heidegger and also to Beckett. This ambivalence of Death is the ultimate problematic. As a result of the prominence of this feature or concept, the curve of the search remains the same but ambiguity enters at the level of authorial intention and a reader can no longer be certain as to whether Beckett is moving from Being through devolution or decreation to Nothingness or from the latter through 'existence' and 'becoming' to the former. Structurally and semantically the text begins, resultantly, to take on a marked post-modern hue since the central argument is being deconstructed. Deferral, ambiguity, and undecidability become the techniques or features of such poems and the very images chosen reveal this complexity. In "Cascando." we see how the pattern has been reversed. The flickering, dying fires of creativity, love, life and memory are pictured in the poem. The other side of 'becoming,' the disturbing hint that life may not be a journey from nothing to something but instead from potential to zero is shown. In "Ooftish," once more a poem about the stress of existence, the note of revolt and rebellion that is metaphysical in origin and felt mainly by the existentialists and nihilists is struck. It is a poem where neither Being (the metaphor for which in the context of the poem is God) nor Nothingness (Death) is glorified. Instead the humanity of Jesus Christ becomes an example, in terms of suffering, of the truth of 'reality' or the intermediary stage between Death and God.

In the poem "they come" the movement is from 'existence' to Being. Love is shown as a metaphor for Being and Beckett records the dismal fact that mankind lives not in love but in its binary opposite, "the absence of love." While this is a discouraging fact to record, the silver lining is that at least most of mankind is not yet swallowed up in the 'hollowness' of hate. Passivity that leads to movement without fruition, symbolized by people coming to the absent protagonist of the poem without gaining in affection, works as an objective correlative for an existence that resembles what the wise King Solomon might have described as 'delusion' and 'vanity,' metaphors for 'mere' nothingness.

"Dieppe" embodies a rejection of Nothingness, the emblem of which is the sea in the poem. "Dieppe" is a poem where the poet surprisingly opts for the positive, active side of the flux of becoming, rejecting the passive, negative side that he usually represents as contemplative in essence. The poem even hints at a hope that Being, called "lights," may eventually be reached by such a choice that turns away from the void, death and the ante-purgatorial impotent life of the philosophic rambler. Poems like this show that Beckett was aware of subtle differences in nuance that could be brought in while dealing with the same structure of meaning.

Watt, the novel that contains quite a few poems or poetic attempts, is a perfect example of the search or the quest. In a journey that is reminiscent of not only Kafka's Joseph K's in *The Castle* but also of John Bunyan's Christians in *Pilgrim's Progress*, Watt, the protagonist and central character of the novel, travels to the house of Knott. One who does not know his worth (What?) seeks understanding or revelation of the same. But on coming face to face with the object of his search who is both a mystery (a {k}not) and a (N)aught/ (N)ought, the result is temporary insanity and in the end resignation to 'existence' as the natural mode of living/dying. The search for Being is frustrated and instead nothingness irradiates the text. *Watt* is a classic parable of the modern man's plight, a state of being that Camustermed "Absurdity"[12] that even the dark writers of our century have found it difficult to adjust to. Nausea and existential angst, dread, despair and even fear and trembling[13] seem inadequate responses to this horrific vision of the insignificance of man's place in the universe. The terrifying note of 'indifference' that creeps into Beckett's narrative seems to him, along with Art, the only weapons with which to explore and stave off the frightening and expanding vision that he has of the Not. The trite pettiness of six of the eight snippets of verse in *Watt* may be the result of this vision and the reaction to it. In "To Nelly," for example, an imprisoned solicitor's idea of Being is seen to be primarily pornographic. He prefers sexual fantasizing to the mere nothingness of spending time in jail for his social misdemeanors. In Arsene's small poem, two seekers are shown. Like words that, combined and varied via repetition and permutation, produce both sense and nonsense the seekers are shown to be sensible or nonsensical depending not on the nobility or unimportance of their quest but on their attitudes.

Stoicism is praised and restlessness damned. The two nearly incoherent threnes heighten nonsense to a pitch of estrangement to describe the tension in Watt's decaying mind that is tormented by the cacophonic and discordant drone of schizophrenic voices but they also spell out a halting message that can be paraphrased to mean roughly what Eliot meant when he spoke of "the stuffed men/the hollow men"[14] in "The Hollow Men." The song of the frogs seems merely inane at first, but one can also view it as Beckett's first tentative attempt to present Nothingness not as a concept but directly, via the exposition of the illegitimacy of language that masquerades as meaningful but may be merely empty. In the song of the frogs, and indeed in the poem "Watt will not," Being also finds its echo or image in the ability of Art to impose 'order' on chaos. Thus frogs in nature croak at random but Beckett's frogs croak at intervals that can be charted mathematically, inscribing an equation of logical progression where melody and harmony are interwoven. The poetics of aesthetics or its reverse redeems the Nothing raising it to a level of significance here. Elsewhere in the novel, the same poetics levels concepts like the idea of 'knowing' to having only about as much significance as the croaks of frogs. In the poem "Watt will not" repetition and variation, permutation and combination and the structure of the gyre interpenetrate to create a moving polyphony of words that instigate poetic Being into awakening, besides working as an excellent gloss on the meaning of this difficult novel. The experiment of writing *Watt* led to Beckett recognizing his literary enterprise for what it was finally. In the memorable poem found in the addenda he states his themes. They would be, as they almost were before without his knowing it fully perhaps, aging, poverty, suffering, ignorance, death and Nothingness. These negative, virginal themes defy expression and his art would consequently be non-expressive. But he would bridle the anguish, or to put it more accurately, "the situation"[15] of non-expression effectively with the help of meta-forms and structures that exist in refined states of pre-composition, where verbs like 'waiting' and prefixes like 'un' signify meanings like 'instability' and hold the centre of the text. The poem declares the coming of age of the post-modernism of Beckett. His poems and texts from then on begin to resemble abstract paintings like those of Jackson Pollock, minimalist music etc. They break free from referentiality and significance to became mimetic of creation not in the Aristotelian sense of representation but in the Platonic or Rimbaudian senses of imitating the very process of creativity so that the work of art comes into its own state of becoming or equilibrium almost as if it were an object with a life of its own. Art of this kind loves serpentine discursivity and convolutedness.

The poems of Beckett since *Watt*, whether they are trifles like the epitaph in "First Love" and the two quatrains that are parodies of the love-poem in *Malone Dies* or serious verse like "Saint-Lô," the three translations from the French of 1947-' 49, the two song-poems in "Words and Music," "dread nay," "Something there," "Roundelay," "thither" or the song of "neither," reveal a flexibility that is involuted but sensitive and able to incorporate the subtlest of vibrations in meaning. The structures at play are Cartesian, dialectical, structural, Kantian, deconstructive, Aristotelian, entropic, that of Nietzschean recurrence or Dantescan. In other words, they exhibit maturity in both the art and the artist. Irrespective of whether the reader is impressed by Beckett, his views and the content of his works, his control over his art reaches the point where it cannot be denied.

Moreover, in these later poems, Beckett begins to play with the structure of the dialectic itself, showing that even with such a basic but limited design it is possible to keep writing, producing both sameness and freshness by introducing slight variations in emphases and possibilities. He proves that depth matters more than width in art either consciously or unconsciously. This proposition can be explained by exposition of his mature poems.

The triadic/dyadic grid of Nothingness-Existence/Becoming/Un-becoming-Being becomes in the later poems of Beckett a framework of portentuousness. In "Saint-Lô", invigorating potency is let in by setting the pattern up in duplication, but in mutual antagonism. The city (the world) is being renewed, rising up from the morass of Nothingness ("havoc"). It is moving — an almost communal thrust is hinted at by the poet to describe the vehemence of the movement — from rubble, wrack and ruin into the richness of existence. The process of rehabilitation, birth or becoming is vividly captured in a few words by the poet. At the same time, the individual (the self) is sinking into death. The tension is created by placing the exciting hope the city has of coming alive against the tragic certainty of the scribe of this historical process of his own mortality. The result is intense. The pattern of the gyre that winds and unwinds simultaneously is again effectively, implicitly present in this poem. Waxing and waning, ebb and flow, the seasonal and cyclical skeleton of Reality . . . the mature poems of Beckett are superb emblems for all these. In the French poems of 1947-'49 they are hauntingly evoked again. In the poems "my way is in the sand flowing" and "what would I do without this world faceless incurious" we have powerful metaphors for existence that can easily be compared in terms of imagery to the best anywhere in world literature. The negative, contemplative zone of 'existence' or 'reality' where 'decay' is the key feature instead of 'germination' is given adequate objective correlatives by Beckett in his choice of images and words. The use of images like the sand — suggestive of the hourglass where time ticks away dismally and cannot be stalled — the shingle, the dune (reminiscent of the desert where life receives very little sustenance), oxymorons like "summer rain" and "its beginning . . . its end" and verbs like "treading" and "receding" makes the poem "my way is in . . . " a classic. And the final image of living "the space of a door/that opens and shuts" with others like "mist," "long-shifting thresholds" and verbs like "harrying fleeing" hint at the multiplicity of the self's being. Interestingly enough it is one of the only poems of Beckett that has been translated, after it was written originally in French, into not only English but also German and Italian. Since the complexity is not language-centred in the Joycean sense, very little seems to have been lost in the process of translation. Something may even have been gained to compensate for any such loss, since Beckett as much at ease in English and these other European languages as he was in French.

The poem "What would I do without this world . . . " is similarly complex. In it Being finds expression as a series of exhilarating nouns. They are "world," "wave," "silence," "succour," "love" and "sky." Nothingness is subjugated or subordinated, but also present in its synonyms "the void" and "ignorance," in verbs like "engulf" and "die" and in the image-symbol-metaphor of the earth as "ballast *dust*" for the "sky" that is metaphorized as a soaring balloon. In the poem 'existence' comes into its own, becoming 'being,' moving beyond the need for definition to a freedom that precludes even the seeming inevitability of and necessity for the terms Being and Nothingness for it to exist. The transitory becomes the vital in a poetic coup de grace that is unforgettable. In the first stanza of the poem the self points out that in a world where to "to be lasts but an instant," acknowledging that the experience of Being even if granted cannot be sustained, existing is also an energetic mode of life. This is suggested by verbs like "spills," "murmurs," "pantings," and "frenzies." Then in the second stanza the self triumphantly asserts that even if suddenly left bereft of or deprived of the alternatives of Being or Nothingness the journey would still continue and existence could still be heightened to a pitch of hope and querulousness, the intensity of which is suggested by the unmatched excellence of the last lines of the poem where it is shown as still "living/in a convulsive space / among the voices voiceless / that throng . . . hiddenness," looking for "another" like it. Becomingness acquires total expression in these memorable lines where existence outruns itself.

The third translated poem in the series "Six Poèmes 1947-'49," "I would like my love to die," while not as powerful as the others, still needs to be remarked on. In it Death gets preference over Love. Being is rejected and Nothingness chosen. But paradoxically enough the choice seems to be made because the narrator holds the view that Love is a state of 'non-being' since it does not seem to actually exist in the mortal realm. Hence, opting for Death is better and in doing this one is opting for Being. One of the elements of Beckett's art that makes it constantly surprising is the absence of fixity in the correspondences between metaphors and what they are supposed to indicate. The correspondences change from period to period. It is this inconsistent approach that makes such poems retain the reader's interest since he wants to find out what the author's position has become. One can say that "I would like my love to die" is a poem closer to "Cascando" in mood and atmosphere than to "Dieppe" where Being is justified as the goal of existence. The difference may have come about due to the change noticed in Beckett since *Watt* that was hinted at in "Cascando," from youthfulness to pessimism. In his later poems he consistently seems to think of Nothingness as more desirable, perhaps because it is more easily attainable in the experience of annihilation (Death), than Being. But the pull is balanced through

Art and he never trips over into being homicidal or suggesting that the way out of suffering the experience of a fading life is suicide or euthanasia. He stems despair by portraying how 'becoming' is momentary and results not in Being but in an unwinding that will result eventually in ashes where the fire of 'existence' once burned bright and clear.

The two poems that appear in Beckett's radio-play "Words and Music" both elicit facets about dying orentering the void that are like sparks of illumination. The first poem "Song," about aging, reports how the untimely memory of the search for love is no solace or substitute for Being. Touching once again on themes hinted at in "Cascando" and "Ooftish," that of the "too late . . . too soon" and of "love requited unrequited," Beckett comments that while existence may be the sphere of romance it is not that of authentic living. In the second poem, Words and Music act as a deadly point and counterpoint to elaborate on death as that "wellhead." Hints as of Buddhist enlightenment, defined by negatives, and the image of labour or pregnancy seen as gradually unfolding from within the womb into birth are placed in the text to suggest the unnerving and apparently beautiful mystery, according to Beckett, of Death. As in "I would like my love to die," 'the void' is foregrounded.

The poems "dread nay" and "Something there" hold the encroaching gulf of Nothingness that perhaps also signifies the onset of artistic barrenness at bay. The image used in "dread nay" for Nothingness is an expanse of white (paper?). The two poems describe flares of becoming that resemble the wake of shooting stars. These brief epiphanies, eructated forth not out of Proustian association but by words, occur against a background where Beckett almost achieves his ambition, repeatedly stated in his journalistic pieces and criticism, of an Art that according to the Belacqua Shuah of *Dream* should state "silences more competently than ever abetter man spangled the butterflies of vertigo."[16] Beckett wrote in a letter in 1937: "Is there any reason why that terrible materiality of the word surface should not be capable of being dissolved, like for example the sound surface, torn by enormous pauses, of Beethoven's seventh symphony, so that through whole pages we can perceive nothing but a path of sounds suspended in giddy heights, linking unfathomable abysses of silence."[17] In "dread nay," and in "Something there" to a lesser extent, this almost happens. In many of the lines of these two poems meaning is absent but hyperactive and the result is an uncanny linking of sounds, silences and images of an instant of becoming (becoming images!?) in the world of not only Time and Space but also the Imagination. The moments of aesthetic revelation in "dread nay" and "Something there" embodied in lines like "asylum head/ sole blot", "sudden in/ ashen smooth/ aghast/ glittering rent" ("dread nay") and "the eye/ opens wide/ wide/ till in the end/ nothing more/ shutters it" ("Something there") are 'framed' by meaninglessness, formlessness, the absence of structure and the counter-tension of the pressure of "unborn" things trembling in longing to come into Being. The result is almost the happening Beckett posited in the same letter of 1937: "In this dissonance between the means and their use it will perhaps become possible to feel a whisper of that final music or that silence "(Nothingness)" "that underlies All"[18] (Being? or vice versa?). If the perfect form for being (or Being) as we know it imperfectly is, as Beckett stated, "an ejaculation[19], these poems attempt to represent that process of shuddering into an entrance and exit almost successfully, not yet as objective correlatives, but as imperfect narratives aspiring to the same and occasionally becoming, in patches, valid aesthetic metonyms of this.

"Roundelay" and "Thither" are better poems than the ones just considered because they do not represent but are expressive of the stasis of existence and the beauty of becoming in their tantalizingly incomplete, photographic finesse. The concept 'Beauty' receives its justification and poetry, literature and Art are suddenly seen in these poems as that mode of labour wherein both the anguish and the failure to inscribe or transcend to Being and the fear or love of Nothingness that may also be a partially Freudian desire for Death can be alchemized. The two-edged sword of living and dying, of coming and going, is shown as still worthwhile by these two fragile poems. The poems speak of linearity but also of recurrence. In their nostalgic and wistful evocation of old age and childhood respectively, where the unsaid speaks as much as, if not more than, the said, they are clearly reminiscent of many Beckettian pieces and also vaguely of Dylan Thomas's bittersweet style. Strangely enough, Wordsworth is also evoked, fittingly, since both these poems have something melancholic about them in true 'Romantic' fashion. Being and Nothingness, while clearly pictured in images in both the poems, do not reign in them.

The last poem to be considered, in this context of discussing what one may call Beckett's major theme if so inclined, is "neither." In it we have the clearest aesthetic exposition and metaphor for all that has been said till now. Cartesian dualism, Hegelian dialecticism, Kant's unknowable 'noumenons,' Heidegger's 'Being,' Sartre's notion of 'non-being' and even deconstructive notations can be sensed to be implicitly at work in this poem. The language has become so transparent that the poem resonates, enabling numerous sensitive interpretations to emerge from its interstices. But Beckett does not limit himself, he extends these positions intelligently. In the poem one finds an impenetrable self (one of Kant's noumenons) and an impenetrable unself (Descartes' 'object' or 'world'). Both could be antithetical in Hegelian terms to one another. They could be metaphors for Being and Nothingness. But in between "falls the shadow,"[20] the state or place of existence, living, becoming, dying and reality. Beckett calls this the "neither." He also calls it the "unspeakable home." This "neither," where someone who is not the self or the other and is not conscious of existing paces, is "unheeded" as yet in art and philosophy, in poetry, literature, aesthetics and critical theory. "It" can be lit up only when the non-self that is also the non-unself halts and absents itself from "the way" it is. Perhaps this may be possible only after Death, the poem suggests. Meanwhile it is possible only to hint at such a process, place, timeless state or flux non-expressively. As in naked repetition where difference plays without one being able to weigh it here too 'the potential for meaning' must be intuited, making the text rich and mysterious in a way very few ancient texts are. In "neither," "the gulf" between Being and Nothingness finally finds "voices voiceless." The philosophy of deconstruction has surely influenced Beckett and helped him to create such metaphysically dis-oriented art. In this poem the strands come together almost like a last "unword."[21] The quest for Being, the search for Nothingness, the presence of the road, the see-sawing journey, 'the cloud of unknowing' that makes not only Being and Nothingness but also existence itself impenetrable and the impersonal voice that still keeps on 'trying' to narrate in the face of such a task or obstacles until no choice is left are all there. One can say that this is both vintage and quintessential Beckett. The virtue of such art is its dogged, unflinching courage and refusal to give in and its lucidity in expressing the aporia it finds itself in.

Why does trying to transcend the roots of resistance in language with the help of non-expression make such a powerful impression on the reader? As Beckett reduces or impoverishes language to the barest of essentials and tropes, concentrating simultaneously on its ineptitude in expressing Being or Nothingness and its aptitude to state this ineptitude, the text into which both Being and Nothingness are unable to enter, epistemologically speaking, becomes a place where ontological pressures/ pleasures flicker nascently. Our teleological longing is subverted and in its place is offered to us a vacuum, a womb or a tomb in which stirs a possibility for "disastrous and" perhaps "immortal worlds."[22] This possibility itself speaks of a chance or chances for abundant fulfilment and absolute failure. The result is an inexplicable sense of metaphysical vastness, a Meaning-shaped void that awaits discovery, invention and exploration and seems inexhaustible to the knowledge-centred. It is also exciting because it is seems to be masterable yet its depths cannot ever be fully sounded.

Non-expression is not a path the artist can pursue without anguish. Consequently, the anguish finds expression in Beckett's poems. In the title "For Future Reference" the anguish is hinted at. It suggests that his work is not yet complete. It seems as if it will never be completed and yet he must toil on. Many of Beckett's works bear this stamp, implying that their roughness and jaggedness must be excused since what is being tried out is more than the feasible. In "Casket of Pralinen . . . " the anguish is clearly verbalized. Beckett writes: "Oh I am ashamed/ of all clumsy artistry/ I am ashamed of presuming/ to arrange words/ of everything but the ingenuous fibres/ that suffer hone stly."In *Echo's Bones*, the title speaks of the possibility of silence or of speech such as that of the "dry bones"[23] of a skeleton. While it can be read as something to be looked forward to, silence can also be a threatening possibility because it can symbolize artistic impotence. The vulture in the first poem, the symbol of the creative thrust, is hungry and "mocked by a tissue that may not serve." In the last poem of the collection, the phrases "muffled revels" and the "gantelope of sense and nonsense" are similarly indicative of the anguish of non-expression seeping through briefly. In the collection of *Echo's Bones* evidence of such aesthetic anguish is not really forthcoming. But it begins to proliferate since "Cascando." In "Cascando," the lines "why not merely the despaired of/ occasion of/ wordshed" and the phrase "saying again" appearing thrice speak for themselves. If this is not enough, the key stanza in the poem: "the churn of *stale* words in the heart again/ love love love thud of the *old* plunger/ pestling the *unalterable* whey of *words*" is also enunciative. In "What would I do. . . " one again finds a plaint against "silence where the murmurs die" and the "voices voiceless," the best metaphors perhaps for Beckett's occasional anguish at his inability to express. In "neither," the word "unspeakable" appears but the anguish has been partly tethered by then. The writer has become resigned to the situation of non-expression and actively opts for the dilemma that this places him in.

What vindicates such art and these poems? It is the 'bridle' that is occasionally seen in them, controlling the angst of non-expression. At one level, this bridle consists of the forms, structures and metonyms that dominate these poems that have been pointed out in this conclusion. At a deeper level, it is in the words, images, music, phrases, lines, stanzas and poems where Beckett is actually able to crystallize into poetry exact metonyms and emblems for reality, life, death, love, living, dying, suffering, sorrow, the absence of love, existence, nothingness, being, etc. Fortunately such moments of poetic Being are not few. Indeed in Beckett's poems they play out a "long night phrase" in "purity quiet." It may be a valid exercise to place a few such moments of transcendence side by side with parallels from the verse of two other modern masters so that one can see and judge for oneself their greatness and intrinsic value, one that for the present reader equals the others.

In *The Waste Land* one comes across these unforgettablelines:

You gave me hyacinths first a year ago;
"They called me the hyacinth girl,"
Yet when we came back, late from the Hyacinth garden
Your arms full and your hair wet, I would not
Speak, and my eyes failed, I was neither
Living nor dead, and I knew nothing
Looking into the heart of light, the silence.[24]
(From "The Burial of the Dead": T.S. Eliot;1.35-41)

In Ezra Pound's "Canto LXXXI" these appear:

there came new subtlety of eyes into my tent
whether of spirit or hypostasis,
but what the blindfold hides
or at carnival

nor any pair showed anger
Saw but the eyes and stance between the eyes
colour, diastasis
careless or unaware it had not the
whole tent's room,
nor was place for the full Eidw's
interpass, penetrate
casting but shade beyond the other lights
sky's clear
night's sea
green of the mountain pool
shone from the unmasked eyes in half-mask's
space.[25] (1. 118-133)

And finally, we read these three sections from Beckett's "Serena I":

on the bosom of the Regent's Park the phlox
crackles under the thunder
scarlet beauty in our world dead fish adrift (1. 3-5)

ah across the way a adder
broaches her rat

white as snow
in her dazzling oven strom of peristalsis
limae labor (1.15-19)

then in the grey hold of the ambulance
throbbing on the brink ebb of sighs[26] (1. 33, 34)

As Octavio Paz once stated: "The poetical word has no substitute. It is not a wish to say something, it is something irrevocably said."[27] In other words, poems, whether by Beckett or not, are their own reason for existence and have to justify their Being by such sparkling moments of illumination or by transcendence of the innate resistance in language to such breakthroughs. Beckett as poet manages, despite his own cynicism that it is possible, one too many times not to enchant and entrance us in his poems.

Notes and References

1. Samuel Beckett, "Whoroscope / Notes," *Collected Poems 1930-78* (London: Calder, 1984) 2.
2. Marjorie Perloff, *The Dance of the Intellect* (New York, Cambridge U.P., 1985)
3. Beckett, "Intercessions by Denis Devlin," *Disjecta* ed. Ruby Cohn (London: Calder, 1983) 94.
4. In Perloff's *The Poetics of Indeterminacy* (New Jersey, Princeton U.P., 1987)
5. Stephen Barker, "Conspicuous Absence: Trace and Power in Beckett's Drama," *Rethinking Beckett* ed. Lance St.John Butler & Robin J. Davis (London: Macmillan, 1990)
6. Beckett, "The Three Dialogues" *Disjecta* 144.
7. Beckett, "Dante ... Bruno. Vico .. Joyce": "Here form is content, content is form" *Disjecta* 27. *Proust*: "Indeed he makes no attempt to dissociate form from content." (New York: Grove P., 1931, 1970) 67.
8. Lance St. John Butler. *Rethinking Beckett.*
9. *Webster's 9th New Collegiate Dictionary* (Masachusetts: Merriam-Webster, 1988) 141.
10. *Webster's* 808.
11. Beckett, "Whoroscope," *C.P.* 4.

12. Albert Camus in Martin Esslin's *The Theatre of the Absurd* (England: Penguin, 1983) 23.
13. Words made of importance to this century by Jean Paul Sartre and Soren Kierkegaard, the chief of the atheistic and theistic existential philosophers.
14. T.S. Eliot, "The Hollow Men," *Selected Poems* (London: Faber, 1982) 76.
15. Beckett, "The Three Dialogues," *Disjecta* 145.
16. Beckett, "Excerpts from Dream...," *Disjecta* 49.
17. Beckett, "Letter to Axel Kaun, 1937," trans. Martin Esslin, *Disjecta* 172.
18. Ibid.
19. Beckett, in Harvey's *Samuel Beckett* 441.
20. T.S. Eliot, "The Hollow Men," *Selected Poems* 80.
21. Beckett, "Letter to Axel Kaun," *Disjecta* 172.
22. Conrad Aiken, "Prelude XIV," *Faber Book of Modern Verse* (London: Faber, 1982) 150.
23. Ezekiel 37.4, *The Authorised Version of the King James Bible* (London: T.B.S, 1990) 808.
24. T.S Eliot, "The Waste Land," *Faber Book of Modern Verse* 123.
25. Ezra Pound "Canto LXXXI," *Faber Book of Modern Verse* 117-18.
26. Beckett, "Serena I," *C.P.* 21,22.
27. Octavio Paz, "Introduction to the History of Mexican Poetry," *Anthology of Mexican Poetry* trans. Beckett (London: Calder & Boyars, 1970)

    All the quotes from Beckett's poems in this chapter, except for the ones from "Serena I," have been left unacknowledged because they have been quoted before in the preceding chapters and the bibliographic details are already given at the end of each of them. If given here too, the end-notes would have become irritatingly unwieldy. Some other quotes have also been dealt with in this manner.

A Select Bibliography

Works by Samuel Beckett

Proust. New York: Grove P., 1970.

More Pricks Than Kicks. London: Calder & Boyars, 1970.

Murphy. London: Picador, 1973.

Watt. New York: Grove P., 1970.

Mercier and Camier. New York: Grove P., 1974.

Molloy. Trans. Beckett and Patrick Bowles. London: Picador, 1979.

Malone Dies. London: Calder & Boyars, 1975.

The Unnamable. New York: Grove P., 1970.

How It Is. London: Calder & Boyars, 1964.

"Neither." *Journal of Beckett Studies* 4 London: Calder, 1979.

Company. London: Calder, 1980.

Disjecta. Ed. Ruby Cohn. London: Calder, 1983. It contains Beckett's important letters and pieces of criticism.

Worstward Ho. London: Calder, 1983.

A Samuel Beckett Reader. Ed. John Calder. London: Picador, 1983.

Collected Poems 1930-1978. 1984. London: Calder, 1986.

Collected Shorter Prose 1945-1980. 1984. London: Calder, 1986. Includes all the important Beckettian 'shorts' in prose.

The Complete Dramatic Works. London: Faber, 1986. It contains all the thirty-two important dramatic works of Beckett.

"Stirrings Still," *The Indian Post*. 19 Mar. 1989.

(The years given are those of the publications of editions used for the purpose of this thesis; not that of composition or first publication. The works are listed chronologically.)

Works on Samuel Beckett

Acheson, James and Kateryna Arthur, eds. *Beckett's Later Fiction and Drama: Texts for Company*. New York: St. Martin's P., 1987.

Butler, Lance St. John & Robin J. Davies. *Rethinking Beckett*. London: Macmillan, 1990.

Alvarez, A. *Beckett*. Glasgow: Fontana, 1981.

Bair, Deirdre. *Samuel Beckett: A Biography*. London: Jonathan Cape, 1978.

Cohn Ruby. *Samuel Beckett: The Comic Gamut*. New Jersey: Rutgers U.P., 1962.

______ ed. *Samuel Beckett: A Collection of Criticism*. New York: McGraw Hill, 1975.

Esslin, Martin, ed. *Samuel Beckett: A Collection of Critical Essays*. New Jersey: Prentice Hall, 1980.

______ . *Beckett at 60: A Festschrift*. London: Calder & Boyars, 1967.

Federman, Raymond and John Fletcher. *Samuel Beckett: His Works and His Critics: An Essay in Bibliography*. California: U. of California P., 1970.

Fletcher, John. *Samuel Beckett's Art*. London: Chatto&Windus, 1967.

______ . *The Novels of Samuel Beckett*. London: Chatto& Windus, 1970.

______ and Beryl S. Fletcher. *A Student's Guide to the Plays of Samuel Beckett* London: Faber, 1985.

Friedman, A, W., et al., eds. *Beckett Translating / Translating Beckett*. London: Pennsylvania U.P., 1986.

Friedman, M. J., ed. *Samuel Beckett Now*. (Chicago: Chicago U.P., 1970.

Graver, Lawrence and Raymond Federman, eds. *Samuel Beckett: The Critical Heritage*. London: Routledge & Kegan Paul, 1979.

Harvey, Lawrence E. *Samuel Beckett: Poet and Critic*. New Jersey: Princeton U.P., 1970.

Jacobsen, Joseph and William R. Mueller. *The Testament of Samuel Beckett*. London: Faber, 1964.

Kenner, Hugh. *A Reader's Guide to Samuel Beckett*. London: Thames & Hudson, 1973.

Knowlson, James., ed. *Happy Days / Oh Les Beaux Jours*. London: Faber, 1978.

Levy, Eric P. *The Voice of Species*. London: Gill & Macmillan, 1970.

Mercier, Vivian. *Beckett / Beckett.* New York: Oxford U.P., 1977.

Pilling, John. *Samuel Beckett.* London: Routledge & Kegan Paul, 1976.

Scott, Nathan A. *Samuel Beckett.* London: Bowes & Bowes, 1965.

General

Abrams, M. H.*A Glossary of Literary Terms.* India: Macmillan, 1978.

Aristotle. *Theory of Poetry and Fine Art.* Trans. S.H. Butcher. U.S.A: Dover, 1951.

Church, Margaret. *Time and Reality: Studies in Contemporary Fiction.* Chapel Hill: The U. of North Carolina P., 1963.

Dante, Alighieri. *La Divina Commedia.* Ed. C.H. Gradgent and Charles S. Singleton. Cambridge: Harvard U.P., 1972.

______ . *The Selected Works.* Ed. Paolo Milano. Trans. Lawrence Binyon. London: Chatto&Windus, 1972.

DesCartes, Rene. *A Discourse on Method: Meditations and Principles.* London: Dent, 1984.

Esslin, Martin. *The Theatre of the Absurd.* England: Penguin, 1983.

Fiebelman, James K. *Understanding Philosophy* Bombay: Jaico Publishing House, 1973.

Gibaldi, Joseph and Walter S. Achert, eds, *MLA Handbook for Writers of Research Papers.* New Delhi: Wiley Eastern, 1988.

Guillen, Jorge. *Language and Poetry.* Cambridge: Harvard U.P., 1961.

Hopkins, G. M. *The Major Poems.* Ed. Walford Davis. London: Dent / Dutton, 1979.

Humphrey, Robert. *Stream of Consciousness in the Modern Novel* California: U. of California P., 1962.

Jackson, W.T.H. *Medieval Literature: A History and a Guide.* New York: Collier, 1967.

Lewis, C. S. *The Allegory of Love.* London: Oxford: U.P., 1950.

Oliver, Egbert S, ed. *American Literature 1890-1965: An Anthology.* New Delhi: Eurasia Publishing House, 1967.

Palgrave, Francis T., ed. *The Golden Treasury of English Songs and Lyrics.* London: Dent, 1955.

Perloff, Marjorie. *The Poetics of Indeterminacy: Rimbaud to Cage* New Jersey: Princeton U.P., 1981.

______ *The Dance of the Intellect: Studies in the Poetry of the Pound Tradition.* New York: Cambridge U.P., 1985.

Pound, Ezra. *Literary Essays of Ezra Pound.* Ed. T.S. Eliot. London: Faber, 1934.

Roberts, Michael and Peter Porter, eds. *The Faber Book of Modern Verse.* London: Faber, 1982.

Sabin, Margery. *The Dialect of the Tribe: Speech and Community in Modern Fiction.* New York: Oxford U.P., 1987.

The Bible. The Authorised King James Version. London: T.B.S., 1990.

The Book of Common Prayer. London: Fontana.

The Concise Oxford English Dictionary. Bombay: Oxford U.P., 1985.

Select Index